THE YEAR I WAS BORN

Compiler Dorothea Duncan

Signpost Books

Published by Signpost Books, Ltd
25 Eden Drive, Headington, Oxford OX3 0AB

First published 1995
10 9 8 7 6 5 4 3 2 1

Based on an original idea by Sally Wood
Conceived, designed and produced by Signpost Books, Ltd
Copyright in this format © Signpost Books, Ltd 1995
Compiler: Dorothea Duncan
Designer: Paul Fry
Editor: Dorothy Wood

ISBN 1 874785 24 4

The moral right of the author has been asserted. All rights reserved.

Acknowledgments: Mirror Group Newspapers plc. for all the pictures in which they hold copyright, and Hugh Gallacher for his invaluable help in retrieving them from the files;Associated Press, pp. 27, 30, 61; Hulton Deutsch Collection, pp. 8, 17, 32, 38, 39, 68, 44, 63, 86; PA News, pp. 47-48, 71, 81.
Every effort has been made to trace all copyright holders, but if any have been inadvertently overlooked, the publishers will be pleased to make the necessary arrangements at the first opportunity.

Printed and bound in Italy.

All rights reserved. Without limiting the rights under copyright reserved above, no part of this publication may be reproduced, stored or introduced into a retrieval system, or transmitted in any form or by any means (electronic, mechanical, photocopying, recording or otherwise), without the prior written permission of both the copyright owners and the above publisher of this book.

Front cover pictures (clockwise, from top): Atom-bomb tests on Bikini Atoll; Manny Shinwell; Celia Johnson and Trevor Howard in *Brief Encounter;* Rudolph Hess at the Nuremberg War Trials; Bananas are back in London after the War.

ME THEN

ME NOW

PERSONAL PROFILE

Names:

Date of Birth:

Place of Birth: **Time of Birth:**

Weight at Birth: **Parents' names:**

Colour of Eyes: **Colour of Hair:**

Distinguishing Marks: **Weight now:**

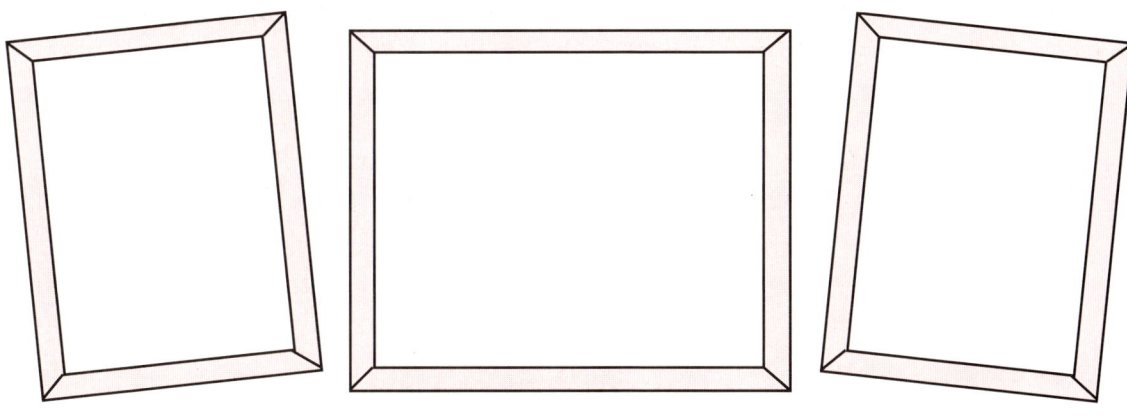

MY FAMILY

JANUARY

THE END FOR LORD HAW-HAW

 **JAN 3** William Joyce, more widely known as Lord Haw-Haw, who was convicted of high treason for his radio broadcasts from Nazi Germany during the war, is hanged at Wandsworth Prison, London.

1 Tuesday
New Year's Day

In the New Year's Honours List, **Winston Churchill** is awarded the Order of Merit; Field Marshals **Lord Alanbrooke**, **Sir Bernard Montgomery** and **Sir Harold Alexander** become viscounts, as do Admiral of the Fleet Lord Cunningham and **Lord Portal**, Marshal of the Air Force. Lord Portal also receives the OM.

■ The 2.50pm Fleetwood to London fish **train collides** with a stationary local passenger train at Lichfield, Staffs – 20 people are killed and 14 injured.

■ London's new **Heathrow Airport** is formally handed over. It will be Britain's largest long-haul flight airport and will cost **£20 million** to build. The first civilian flight to take off, a Lancastrian Star Light captained by Air Vice Marshal Donald Bennett (creator and head of the RAF Pathfinder force), is a test flight to Montevideo for British S American Airways.

2 Wednesday

In a New Year message to his people, **Emperor Hirohito** of

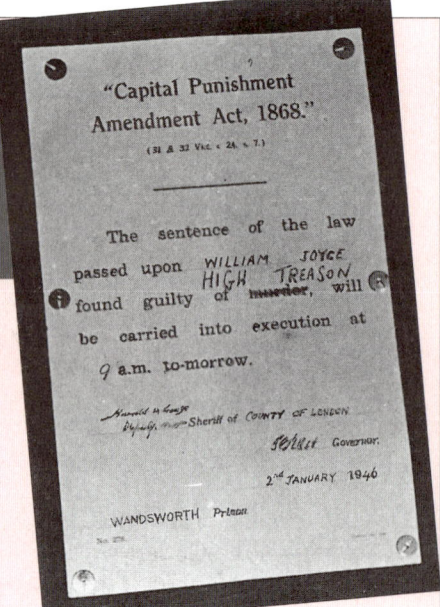

Japan (*bottom*) decrees that he is **not a god**, and that his subjects are not divinely destined to rule the world. For the first time he mentions the word 'defeat' in referring to the recent war.

■ *The Times* readers are asked to post their old copies to the Director of Air Force Welfare, who will distribute them to the RAF in Germany, the Middle East, SE Asia, W Africa and elsewhere.

■ **The Tower of London** reopens to the public, though the crown jewels are not there. The Tower received 15 direct hits during the war, but there was no substantial damage.

3 Thursday
New Moon

BIRTHDAYS: Clement Attlee is 63 today, and Herbert Morrison is 68.

■ The Chief of the UNRRA commission to Greece says that many people in isolated areas of the country will have to live on **bread and water** until April. The TB rate is 15 times as high as it is in the UK.

■ The British Medical Association, which has a membership of 51,310, is trying to get its own MPs into Parliament to monitor the Government's new **National Health Service** proposals.

JANUARY

4 Friday

10,000 **evacuated** children can't return home, either because there is no room for them or because they are orphans. They will remain where they are in the care of the local authorities.
■ The **telephone** service to Luxembourg is extended from today to include social calls. The minimum price is 8s. for 3 min.
■ A joint Anglo-American Committee is set up to consider what steps should be taken in regard to Palestine, and to ease the situation of Jews on the Continent.
. . . DENMARK will reimburse Britain for over £300,000 sent to Denmark for use by the Danish Resistance during World War II . . .

5 Saturday

Mrs McCormack (90) of Carrick-on-Shannon, Leitrim, Eire, finds a fox holding one of her prize turkeys in its mouth when she investigates noises in her hen-house. Outraged, she grabs the fox by its tail, drags it to the kitchen and jams its tail in the door to await her son's return. She receives a reward of 8s. – Shannon County Agricultural Committee's prize for the despatch of foxes.
■ The first **gift of food** from the Lord Mayor of Adelaide's appeal leaves Australia for Britain. It is the largest gift ever sent and includes honey, jam, canned and dried fruit, malted milk pudding and tinned meat.

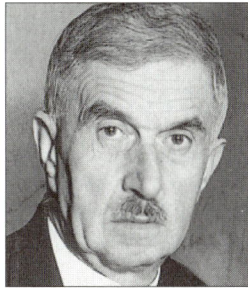

■ **RAIL CRASH:** The 11.15pm King's Cross to Newcastle sleeper express runs into derailed wagons of a goods train nr Ferryhill, Co Durham. Ten people are killed, and 18 injured. The Home Secretary, **Mr Chuter Ede** (left) is on board but isn't injured.

6 Sunday

Dr Clifford Adams, Director of **Marriage** Counselling Services of Pennsylvania State College, USA, offers Hints on How to Make Love in the current *American Magazine* to readers who fear they have lost the art in 4yrs of war.

■ **Brides** of US servicemen and their babies are living in two hotels in Bournemouth while waiting to sail to join their husbands.
■ **Australia** will increase shipments of food-stuffs to Britain from 700,000 tons (1945) to 1,000,000 tons, including 1,500,000 bushels of apples, 1,000,000 cases canned fruit, 275,000 tons frozen canned meat, 60,000 tons butter, 12,000 tons cheese, and 380,000,000 eggs. Australia will 'scrape the bottom of her wheat bins' to meet Britain's needs.

7 Monday

Due to a massive **increase in crime** in London, policemen are being asked to volunteer for 8hrs extra paid duty each week.
■ The famous motor racing track at **Brooklands** (above) is sold to Vickers Armstrong for £330,000.
■ The **Duke of Windsor** is staying with his mother at Marlborough House. He will see the King and attend to private business matters. He dines with Sir Winston and Lady Churchill.
■ The pressure on Britain's **maternity** hospitals is now so great that Dr S Left, medical officer of health in Tottenham, London, urges women to book a bed as soon as they marry.

8 Tuesday

The trial of the **Nazi war criminals** Goering and von Ribbentrop opens in Nuremberg.

JANUARY

■ A public radio telegraph service to British and foreign ships throughout the world is reintroduced at 1s. per word (6d. for ships regularly engaged on short voyages to and from the British Isles).
■ The lake in St James's Park, London, is drained so that a bomb disposal unit can begin work on an **unexploded bomb** that fell near the bridge 5yrs ago.
■ All women in the armed forces may obtain immediate release if they volunteer to become nurses, whether or not they have any previous nursing experience.

9 Wednesday

Winston Churchill leaves London for Florida, after his doctor advises complete rest in a warm climate. **Anthony Eden** takes over as Leader of the Opposition.
■ Something like 10% of **marriages** in Britain are breaking down, says the Marriage Guidance Council. Before long, one in five will break down.
■ Delegates from 51 countries are attending the first meeting of the United Nations Assembly in London. The State gold dinner service is brought out for the first time in years when the King gives a **State Banquet** at St James's Palace.

greeted by a gold map encircled by olive branches. Nearly 1,000 delegates represent 51 nations.
■ **Arab leaders** meet in Jerusalem to consider Britain's request that they admit 6,000 Jews at a rate of 1,500 a month, but declare that no more Jews should be admitted into **Palestine**.
■ The US Army Signal Corps at Evans Signal Laboratories, Belmar, New Jersey, bounce a **radar** signal off the **moon**. The echo takes 2.4 secs to return to earth – a round trip of about 480,000 miles.

10 Thursday

The first ever **UN General Assembly** meeting opens at Central Hall, Westminster, London (*below*) which has been spruced up for the occasion. In the hall the delegates are

11 Friday

Albania is declared a People's Republic. Ex-**King Zog** and his family will live in Britain.
■ Lincoln Cathedral's copy of **Magna Carta** (*above*) housed for safekeeping in the Library of Congress, Washington, comes home. It was sent to New York in 1939 for the World Fair and stayed. It has been seen by 15 million people.
■ **Douglas Bader**, DSO, DFC, famous British air ace who managed to fly even though he has artificial legs, retires from the RAF with the rank of Wing Commander.
. . . It's the warmest January night on record. At Kew the thermometer didn't drop below 52.4°F, the average for June . . .

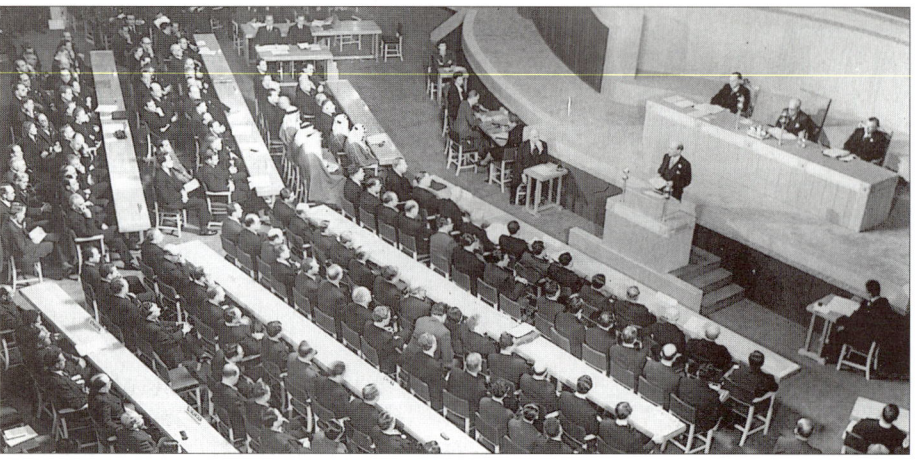

JANUARY

12 Saturday

Crooner **Frank Sinatra** (*right*) is asking for a fee of £2,500 plus free trans-Atlantic air travel, for a series of concerts in Britain in July.
■ A card **posted** in Dublin on July 1, 1936, has just been delivered unsoiled in Portsmouth.
■ 600,000 men are idle in strike-ridden America. Other **strikes** are threatened by 200,000 electrical and 300,000 meat industry workers.

13 Sunday

World War II cost the world's treasuries £170,000,000,000 – almost four times as much as the 1914-18 war.
■ Polish soldiers are taking the place of demobbed British soldiers in the **Orkneys** where they are restoring the islands to their pre-war condition.
■ Church **organists** are demanding higher wages. Some of them get only 6s. a week.
. . . *A jetty on the River Hooghly, Calcutta, India, collapses during a Hindu religious festival. 140 pilgrims are killed . . .*

14 Monday

No. 16 . . . Arsenal, will play . . . Seventy-odd years of secrecy is lifted when the 4th round draw for the **FA Cup** is broadcast from the Council Chamber of the Football Association.
■ A member of the **House of Keys**, Isle of Man, suggests giving a pair of silk stockings and a bonus of £20 to each nurse who stays for a year, to relieve an acute shortage of nurses.

15 Tuesday

Miss Dorothy Knight Dix (36), a London barrister, is the **first woman** in British history to become a **judge.** She has the power to try everything but murder, manslaughter or treason.

■ Hobble skirts, with elastic at the knees, turn up at a fashion parade in London.
■ The principle of **equal pay for women** has been accepted and embodied in a new charter for the British Furniture trade, employing 150,000 workers.

16 Wednesday

British **shipyards** are working under full pressure on 1,612,810 tons of new merchant shipping. Three are liners, but the biggest order is for heavy cargo vessels.
■ **Sir Lewis Casson**, the actor and producer, says the serious theatre is being kept alive almost entirely by the attendance of women.
. . . *8,000 British cars will be imported by New Zealand this year . . .*

17 Thursday
Full Moon

The **UN Security Council**, the chief organ of the UN and 'the organisational bulwark against war and aggression', whose permanent members are the UK, USA, France, USSR, China, plus 6 non-permanent members, convenes in London.
■ An **RAF Lancaster** sets a new record of 32hr 21min from Britain to Cape Town, and a record for the first non-stop Cairo-Cape Town flight of 20hr 37min.
■ A French army officer and his English wife appear in court in Richmond, Surrey, on charges involving Customs and Excise claims of £20,000. They have 812 bottles of French perfume in their house.

18 Friday

A coal merchant, charged with giving **short weight** to customers, is sentenced to 4 months' hard labour at Birmingham Assizes.
■ A boat carrying over 900 illegal Jewish **immigrants** trying to reach Palestine is

7

JANUARY

escorted into Haifa by a British destroyer. The passengers are then transferred to Athlit Camp, where they await the British government's decision on their future.

19 Saturday

30,000 rugger fans see **Scotland** beat the NZ Army touring team at Murrayfield by 11-6. They are the first team to beat the Kiwis on this tour, and the first ever Scottish team to beat a New Zealand side.
■ **SOCCER:** England play Belgium at Wembley and win 2-0. Fog descends in the second half and the surface is frozen, but nothing can dim the gala mood of **Stanley Matthews** (*above*), who celebrates his 44th cap.
. . . **LORD GODDARD is appointed the new Lord Chief Justice, succeeding Viscount Caldecote** . . .

20 Sunday

The Belgian government refuses King Leopold's request that they hold a **referendum** to decide whether he should return to the throne. **Leopold** says he will only abdicate if it goes against him.
■ The English Rugby League international touring team on its way to Australia is to travel on a **'brides' ship'** (a ship carrying the British wives of Australian servicemen). It is the only accommodation available.

21 Monday

Following his withdrawal as head of the French government yesterday, **General de Gaulle** leaves Paris after recording a farewell speech to the French nation.
■ The *News Chronicle* celebrates its centenary. Founded as *The Daily News*, for a short time it was edited by Charles Dickens.
■ Allied troops in Tokyo take over 349 industrial plants, army and naval arsenals and institutes of technical research, as a first instalment of **reparations** in kind. Most of the factories manufacture aeroplane engines, parts and machine tools.
■ 197,000 Hamburg schoolchildren aged 3-6 will receive a hot meal each day as a result of a combined British, Swedish and German Red Cross and Hamburg schools scheme. The food will ensure that each child receives an extra 2000 calories per week.

22 Tuesday

From June 1 **radio licences** will go up from 10s. to £1. Combined radio and TV licences are to be introduced at £2.
■ During the next four months, people in Essex villages will be able to see popular **films** for 1s. 6d. each. It is an experiment to try and keep them at work in the villages and stop the drift to the towns.
■ Recent American films will be shown to **UN conference** delegates in London at the Plaza Theatre at 9.45pm, on Mondays, Wednesdays and Fridays throughout the conference.
. . . **Pit owners protest at the Government's plans to nationalise the coal industry** . . .

23 Wednesday

The UN Assembly creates the **Atomic Energy Commission** to deal with the problems raised by the discovery of atomic energy and its development for both peaceful and destructive purposes.
■ The British **Labour Party** rejects the Communist Party's new application for affiliation.
■ Thomas Barry of Miami, Florida, USA, who is homeless, solves his housing problem by buying a **hearse** and sleeping in the coffin container behind the driver's seat.

8

JANUARY

LOOK WHO WAS BORN THIS YEAR...

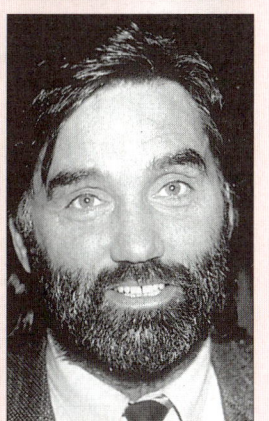

Jan 5	**Dianne Keaton**	Actress
Jan 19	**Dolly Parton**	Singer
Feb 2	**Farrah Fawcett**	Actress
Mar 14	**Jasper Carrott**	Comedian
April 5	**Jane Asher**	Actress
April 17	**Clare Francis**	Yachtswoman
April 18	**Hayley Mills**	Actress
May 1	**Joanna Lumley**	Actress
May 9	**Candice Bergen**	Actress
May 10	**Maureen Lipman**	Actress
	Donovan	Singer
May 22	**George Best**	Footballer
May 28	**Cher**	Singer/actress
June 14	**Barry Manilow**	Singer
June 21	**Maurice Saatchi**	Businessman
July 6	**Sylvester Stallone**	Actor
July 9	**Ilie Nastase**	Tennis player
July 26	**Helen Mirren**	Actress
Sept 13	**Jacqueline Bisset**	Actress
Sept 28	**Helen Shapiro**	Singer
Oct 4	**Susan Sarandon**	Actress
Oct 10	**Charles Dance**	Actor
Oct 13	**Edwina Currie**	Politician
Nov 6	**Sally Field**	Actress
Dec 5	**Jose Carreras**	Singer
Dec 12	**Emerson Fittipaldi**	Racing driver
Dec 20	**Uri Geller**	Illusionist

BIRTHDAY BOYS (and Girls): Top: Charles Dance, Helen Mirren. Above: Dolly Parton, George Best. Top right: Joanna Lumley. Below, left to right: Sylvester Stallone, Cher, Barry Manilow, Susan Sarandon.

JANUARY

■ The Yugoslav government has begun a mass expulsion of Germans. 4,500 have so far arrived in Vienna in spite of Anglo-American protests over the difficulty of housing and feeding the refugees.

24 Thursday

The Government publishes the **National Insurance Bill** as a White Paper. The Government wants to bring part of the scheme, including sickness, unemployment, retirement, maternity grants etc. in this Autumn. Compulsory contribution rates will be 2s.2d. to 4s.7d. for the employed and 1s.9d. to 3s.10d. for employers.
■ **Horse racing** is getting back to normal. For the first three months of the 1946 flat season (begins April 1), there will be racing on 102 days on 29 courses.

25 Friday

After a 6yr rest, Antarctic **whales** are again being hunted. Most of this season's catch will not be used for oil but for feeding the peoples of Europe.
■ RAF men on strike at Almaza aerodrome nr. **Cairo** say they mean to stay out until they hear that their demob date has been brought forward. The strike is already disrupting troop plane services from India.
■ Britain's Ministry of Food has bought 40% (46,000 tons) of the Canary Islands **banana** crop, to begin shipping in February.

26 Saturday

Foundation Day, Australia

France beats Ireland by 4-3 at Lansdowne Road, Dublin. It's the first rugby international

BRITAIN'S GOING BANANAS AT LAST!

DATELINE: January 27
The first consignment of bananas (96,000 stems) for London is being unloaded at West India Docks

since 1938, and the first game Ireland have played against France for 15yrs.
■ A new 3-way **shoe** is a coupon saver. It can be a high-heeled classic court to wear with a tailored suit; clip on a couple of rosettes or frothy pompons and it becomes a dressy little shoe to wear with an afternoon dress; or add a hand-painted bow or dainty cameo clips for evening wear.
■ More than 2,000 angry RAF **airmen go on strike** in India, Ceylon and Singapore protesting about the slow rate of demobilisation.

27 Sunday

England will play home Test matches with India this summer, with S Africa, Australia, N Zealand and the West Indies in succeeding years.
■ Skeletons of a Saxon warrior and a woman of the 6th century have been found below the 14th century Clock House at Lenham, Kent.
. . . 35,000 children fill St Peter's, Rome, to give thanks for RATIONS from UNRRA . . .
■ A US Army P80 crosses the United States from Long Beach, California, to New York in a new **record** time of 4hr 13min. The pilot says he sometimes flew at speeds of up to 660mph.

28 Monday

The prospect of a **National Theatre** is brought closer with the merging of the Shakespeare Memorial, the National Theatre and Old Vic committees. £50,000 has been collected towards a site on the Surrey side of the Thames, and an appeal for £500,000 launched.

FEBRUARY

- A Pan-American **Constellation** aircraft, (right) sets a new record flying from New York to Lisbon in 9hr 58 min.
- British Nylon Spinners say that **nylon stockings** will be on the market in June, and that by summer yarn sufficient to provide 300,000 pairs per week will be produced.
- Two Oldham, Lancs, **cotton mills** stop production because there is no coal.

29 Tuesday

The 11-nation UN Security Council unanimously recommends that **Trygve Lie** (below) the Norwegian Foreign Minister, should be appointed Secretary General of the United Nations.
- The Rugby Union announce the return of **international rugby**, and that English, Scottish, Welsh and Irish caps will be awarded for the 1946-47 season.
- Death of Harry L Hopkins (56), adviser to US Presidents. Roosevelt summoned him to Washington to become one of the prime administrators of the New Deal, and he was Administrator of **Lend-Lease**.

30 Wednesday

Payments of the first **Family 'five-bob' Allowances** will begin on August 6. The scheme is estimated to affect 4,500,000 children.

- The **Nuffield Foundation** has offered Cambridge University £30,000, with a possible further £18,000, to investigate the causes of ageing.
- The longest flight **BOAC** offers is the 'Kangaroo' run to Australia and New Zealand. The fare: £240.
- Britain is to allow Jewish immigration into **Palestine** to continue at the rate of 1,500 per month, but illegal immigrants will be deducted from the quota. This will allow the release of the 900 illegal immigrants detained in a camp since their capture on Jan 18.

31 Thursday

British troops will be part of the first contingent of the Commonwealth **Occupation Force** in Japan. They will arrive at Kure from Hong Kong on Feb 1.
- **Gracie Fields**, star of stage, screen and radio, arrives in the UK for a visit after 4½ years in Italy.
- **Field Marshal Viscount Montgomery** is to become Chief of the Imperial General Staff, the highest appointment in the British Army.
- An Avro York airliner from Johannesburg, opening a new double service between South Africa and London, is stranded in Nairobi by a plague of **locusts**. On landing a number of locusts were drawn into the air-intake and broke a pipe in the radiator. A new radiator is on its way from South Africa.

FEBRUARY

1 Friday

The cost of an air flight from London to Paris by British European Airways is to be £7. It will cost £8.10s to fly to Amsterdam.
- Boulogne harbour opens to cargo traffic with the UK. It is hoped work on the larger docks will be completed by May to allow the

11

FEBRUARY

Films of the

INGRID BERGMAN has audiences spellbound, with three new films this year – including the highly successful Hitchcock thriller, *Spellbound (right)*. **She also stars in** *Saratoga Trunk (far right)* **with Gary Cooper, and** *The Bells of St Mary's*, **with Bing Crosby. The biggest British offering is** *Brief Encounter (opposite page),* **starring Celia Johnson and Trevor Howard. Two more British actors, David Niven and Roger Livesey, find further fame with** *A Matter of Life and Death (bottom, right).* **Charles Dickens'** *Great Expectations* **translates wonderfully to the big screen with John Mills, Valerie Hobson** *(below, left),* **and Martitia Hunt. Larry Parks** *(below, centre)* **stars as Al Jolson in** *The Jolson Story*, **with Evelyn Keyes.**

FEBRUARY

YEAR

Anchors Aweigh	Frank Sinatra, Gene Kelly, Kathryn Grayson
Saratoga Trunk	Gary Cooper, Ingrid Bergman
The Bells of St Mary's	Bing Crosby, Ingrid Bergman
Brief Encounter	Trevor Howard, Celia Johnson
The Corn Is Green	Bette Davis, Emlyn Williams
The Postman Always Rings Twice	Lana Turner, John Garfield
The Captive Heart	Michael Redgrave, Rachel Kempson
The Virginian	Joel McCrea
Gilda	Glenn Ford, Rita Hayworth
The Blue Dahlia	Alan Ladd, Veronica Lake
Spellbound	Gregory Peck, Ingrid Bergman
Make Mine Music	Disney cartoon
Piccadilly Incident	Michael Wilding, Anna Neagle
Anna and the King of Siam	Rex Harrison, Irene Dunne
Night and Day	Cary Grant, Alexis Smith
The Overlanders	Chips Rafferty
A Matter of Life and Death	David Niven, Roger Livesey
The Outlaw	Jane Russell
Great Expectations	John Mills, Valerie Hobson, Jean Simmons
The Big Sleep	Humphrey Bogart, Lauren Bacall
The Jolson Story	Larry Parks
The Kid from Brooklyn	Danny Kaye
Mildred Pierce	Joan Crawford
Les Enfant du Paradis	Arletty, Jean-Louis Barrault

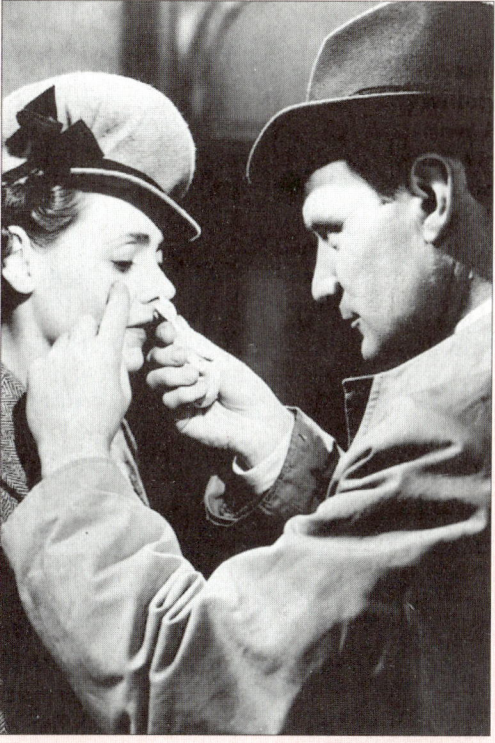

THE BIG SLEEP

Humphrey Bogart, playing the down-at-heel detective Philip Marlowe, teams up with Lauren Bacall in the highly successful Howard Hawks' film *The Big Sleep*.

13

FEBRUARY

resumption of passenger traffic.
■ **Yugoslavia** unveils its new Republican constitution. **General Tito** becomes army C-in-C and forms a new government.
■ Supreme Allied HQ in Tokyo announces that the final casualties caused by the **Hiroshima bomb** were 129,558 (78,150 killed, 13,983 missing, 9,248 seriously injured, 27,997 slightly injured). Another 176,987 were made homeless or suffered sickness from the after-effects.

2 Saturday
New Moon

Ad in the personal column of a Surrey newspaper: *Person wanted for queuing once a fortnight, 6.30am to 9.30am, 1s.6d. an hour. Fare to London paid.*
■ The allocation of domestic **dried eggs** ends today. The Ministry of Food says it is doing what it can to obtain a sufficient supply to resume issue, even on a limited scale, to housewives.
■ 'Snatch bags' is the nickname of a **burglar** being hunted by London police. He steals the trousers and skirts of his victims so they cannot chase him.

3 Sunday

A newly-developed technique of broadcasting **TV in full colour** is demonstrated by CBC in America.
■ **Jane Russell** has Hollywood's perfect pair of legs, says the President of the Hosiery Designers of America. Her measurements are: ankle 8½in, calf 12in and thigh 19½in.
■ The 14th anniversary of non-stop variety at the **Windmilll Theatre** is celebrated with a special show in aid of the Charing Cross Hospital.
■ Three complete 1,000-bed **hospitals**, including medical supplies, are to be sent to Poland from the US Army Depot at Honeybourne, Glos.

4 Monday

Because of the world shortage of **wheat**, bread is to be darker but it will be more nutritious. The amount of flour extracted from wheat is to be raised from 80% to 85%. The outlook in the Far East is grim. Millions will be without wheat or rice.
■ The Egyptian government demands the complete **evacuation** of British troops.
. . . Six Tory MPs table a Commons motion urging the importation of food from America before films . .

5 Tuesday

The London County Council passes the £45 million plan for **rebuilding** the Stepney and Poplar districts of London's East End. It will take 30yr to complete and covers 1,960 acres.
■ Suffolk Council is considering allowing **racehorses** to travel in either direction on streets in Newmarket limited to one-way traffic.
■ There is a prolonged **drought** in India, the worst in the Punjab for 50yrs. The food deficit for the year is estimated at 3,000,000 tons. Only rain will prevent a major calamity.
■ Distinguished stage star **George Arliss** (77), who toured the USA with Mrs Patrick Campbell in 1901 and decided to stay there to become the star of films such as *Disraeli*, *The Man Who Played God* and *Man of Affairs*, dies at his home in London.

6 Wednesday

There is a great rush for FA Cup-tie **tickets**. The normal staff in clubs are so overwhelmed that the footballers are helping out.

FEBRUARY

1946 FACT FILE

World Population	2,147,000,000 (est 1940)
UK Population (GB and N Ireland)	48,106,000
World's largest city - London	8,203,952
UK area (including Irish Free State)	121,463 sq miles
Head of State	King George VI
Prime Minister	**Richard Clement Attlee** (pictured below)
House of Commons	Lab 393; Con 189; Lib 12; Lib National 13; National 14, ILP 3; Communist 1; Scot Nat 2; Ulster Nat 2, Irish Nat 2
UK Births	954,400
UK Deaths	567,027
UK Marriages	441,000
UK Divorces	36,457
Astronomer Royal	Sir Harold Spencer Jones
Poet Laureate	John Edward Masefield
Master of the King's Music	Sir Arnold Trevor Bax
Licensed Motor Vehicles	2,581,027 registered cars
Number of Telephones	2,987,065
Hottest Day	July 12 88°F
Coldest Day	December 21 19°F
NOBEL PRIZE WINNERS	
Peace Prize (2)	Emily Greene Balch (USA)
	John R. Mott (USA)
Literature	Herman Hesse (Ger)

■ The Government steps in to stop the call-up of 8,000 agricultural workers, as the **agricultural** industry has greater need of them than the armed forces.

■ Sir Charles Vyner Brooke (72) the third and last white **Rajah of Sarawak**, whose ancestor the explorer and soldier Sir James Brooke was given the title of Rajah and the kingdom of Sarawak by Rajah Muda Hassim of Borneo for helping him crush a rebellion of Dayak tribes in 1841, cedes Sarawak (Borneo) to Britain.

 Thursday

The Emergency Economic Committee for Europe say that 140 million Europeans will have to live on a **diet** averaging less than 2,000 calories per day – less food than they need to be able to work effectively, and there is the danger of disease. Worst affected are non-farming populations.

■ New York's Mayor O'Dwyer declares a **state of emergency** following the refusal of tug boat employees to end their strike. Street lighting returns to its wartime level of dimness, and Broadway is blacked out.

 Friday

Ashby de la Zouch, the ancient Leicestershire town (pop. 6,000) becomes one of the joke towns of England after the ITMA song which says the 'Skies are full of blue, and cows are full of moo at Ashby de la Zouch by the sea'. Council Chairman Leonard Marshall says, 'It's a downright shame. We've the finest grammar school in the country, and some of the best brains in our universities come from Ashby de la Zouch.'

■ The first **cars** and vans produced in Eire since the war come off the production line at Ford's factory at Cork.

15

FEBRUARY

GI BRIDES ARRIVE

After months of waiting, the first GI brides finally arrive in the USA, to be greeted by their delighted husbands. But not all the brides were lucky . . . some arrived to find their husbands already had a wife, or had disappeared with no forwarding address. These pictures show the happier side. *Left:* **Kenneth Jones** saw the picture of a beautiful girl in a wheelchair in the US forces paper *Stars and Stripes*. He wrote to her, met her and married her, and now he's meeting her off the *Queen Mary*.
Centre: **GI bride Mrs Robertson** and her daughter **Joan Atkins** go aboard the *Queen Mary* for their trip to the USA.
Right: **GI husbands** waiting on the dock to meet 1,048 wives and 376 children who have just arrived from England.

■ Film star **Deanna Durbin**, the star of *100 Men and a Girl, Spring Parade* and other wartime hits, gives birth to a daughter.

9 Saturday

9.45 pm Kings Cross-Newcastle express runs into **derailed** coaches of 9.32am Hatfield-Kings Cross suburban train, which ran into the buffers at Potters Bar. Two are killed, 11 injured. The 5pm Bradford-Kings Cross train then collides with the wreck as it could not be brought to a standstill in time, but no one is hurt.

■ Canada cuts its **butter ration** from 6oz per person to 4oz per person to help maintain the supplies of cheese to Britain and evaporated milk to liberated Europe.
. . . In the rugby international, ENGLAND beat Ireland by 14-6 – their first match in 7yrs.

10 Sunday

The first of 2,300 **GI brides** arrive in New York *(see panel, above).*
The International Union against Race Prejudice, whose organisers are all former concentration camp victims, elect

16

FEBRUARY

IN A NEW WORLD...

Mrs **Eleanor Roosevelt**, the wife of the US president, as their president.

11 Monday

The rush to **learn to drive** is so great that a leading school of motoring is increasing the number of its schools from 15 to 150.
■ The RSPCA have warned Mr Lawrie Jackson of Somerset that they will oppose his plan to establish **mouse racing** as a sport.
■ **Emmanuel Shinwell**, Minister of Fuel and Power, agrees on a nation-wide standardisation of voltage, at 240 volts.
■ There is a severe **earthquake** in Algeria. 276 people are dead and 70 injured.

12 Tuesday

From August, students at Teacher Training colleges will receive **free tuition**. Those whose parents earn less than £300 p.a. will also be eligible for free board.
■ Mr Ralph L Smith of Missouri, USA, pays an amazing 14,500gns for the champion shorthorn bull *Pittodrie Upright*

FEBRUARY

at the Perth sales in Scotland – nearly double the previous world record price.
■ While refacing one of the bunkers at St Andrews Old Course, the head greenkeeper finds an **old golf ball** of the hammered gutta type. It bears the name W Dunn of Musselburgh, and is at least 100yrs old. It is now in the Royal & Ancient club museum.

13 Wednesday

A bill to repeal the Trades Disputes Act of 1927, which banned **general strikes**, has its second reading in the House of Commons and is passed by 369 votes to 194.
■ At his trial for treason in the USA, American poet **Ezra Pound** (60), who broadcast enemy propaganda from Italy to the USA during the war, is declared mentally unsound and unfit to stand trial. He's sent to hospital for investigation and treatment.
■ **Winston Churchill**, on holiday in Miami, Florida, poses for a portrait by Douglas Chandor after President Truman tells him that it was Franklin Roosevelt's wish that paintings of the 'Big Three' (Roosevelt, Churchill and Stalin) should hang side by side in the Capitol, Washington.

14 Thursday
St Valentine's Day

The **Bank of England** is nationalised.
■ First session of the **UN General Assembly** closes.
■ IBM introduces the fast electronic digital computer **ENIAC** (Electronic Numerical Integrator & Computer), which uses 18,000 electronic valves and 1,500 relays. This electronic brain is capable of doing in seconds calculations that would take a human brain hours.
■ In a House of Commons debate on the **food shortage** farmers are asked to cultivate at least the same acreage in 1946 as in 1945, and members of Women's Land Army will be asked to remain on the land. At least 50% of agricultural workers in the Forces should have returned by the end of April,

. . . The International Olympic Committee announces that Britain will host the 1948 Olympic Games – the first since the Berlin Olympics in 1936 . . .

15 Friday

Typhoid is sweeping across Eastern Europe and has reached Berlin, says UNRRA.
■ **Dr Julian Huxley** (left) former secretary of the Zoological Society, London (1935-42) and author of *The Science of Life* (with H G Wells), *Evolution: The Modern Synthesis* and *Evolutional Ethics*, is appointed Secretary General of UNESCO.
■ The Ministry of Food

BOOKS OF THE YEAR

TITUS GROAN	Mervyn Peake
PRIVATE ANGELO	Eric Linklater
WESTWOOD	Stella Gibbons
LORD HORNBLOWER	C S Forester
KING JESUS	Robert Graves
THE RIVER	Rumer Godden
THE OTHER SIDE	Storm Jameson
THIEVES IN THE NIGHT	Arthur Koestler
BRIGHT DAY	J B Priestley
DUNKERLEYS	Howard Spring
PRATER VIOLET	Christopher Isherwood
THE GREAT DIVORCE	C S Lewis
THE WHITE TOWER	James Ramsay Ullman
HIROSHIMA	John Hersey
ENEMY COAST AHEAD	Guy Gibson
A HISTORY OF WESTERN PHILOSOPHY	Bertrand Russell

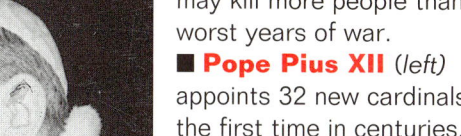

has ordered 300,000 cases of skinned rabbits from Australia and NZ, representing 18 million pounds of meat.

16 Saturday
Full Moon

Russia uses the **veto** for the first time in the UN Security Council debate on Lebanon and Syria.
■ The people of Luton, Beds, vote in favour of **Sunday cinema opening** by 14,825 to 7,906.
■ Decorators discover a **tombstone** dated 1727 with the inscription *'Evan Ellis: a pleasant son of Adam,'* as part of the stone floor of the telephone exchange at Bala, Merioneth.
■ **Swimsuits** in smart designs will be in the shops this summer as manufacturers have been granted a yarn allocation. Prices will range from 7s.10d. to 9s.5d.

17 Sunday

Priests gabbling prayers, giving the impression of boredom, is cited as one reason why people don't go to church.
■ Egypt's new Prime Minister, **Ismael Sidky Pasha**, writes to King Farouk saying he hopes to name a minister to negotiate with Britain over Egyptian independence.
■ Enough **tea** to make 1,000 million cups reaches Britain from Ceylon.
■ Maiden flight of the **Douglas DC6** in Los Angeles, USA. The plane will carry 52 passengers, and Douglas expects to begin delivery to US Airways and the Australian National Airways within the next few weeks.

18 Monday

The Minister of State, Hector McNeil, says that **world famine** in the next 12 months may kill more people than the worst years of war.
■ **Pope Pius XII** (*left*) appoints 32 new cardinals. For the first time in centuries, the Italians will be outnumbered 42 to 27.
■ **Rescue** workers in the five villages of the province of Setif, Algeria, devastated by last Monday's earthquake, report 327 dead and 250 injured, but the numbers are still rising.

19 Tuesday

The Army has good news for the **Aintree racecourse** authorities – the course will be handed back to them on March 1, in time for the Grand National to be run on its traditional turf a month later.
■ The Theatre Royal, Bristol, believed to be the oldest theatre in the country, begins a new chapter tonight when the newly formed Bristol Old Vic co-premieres Farquhar's restoration comedy *The Beaux' Stratagem*.
■ London concert manager Harold Fielding cancels **Frank Sinatra**'s British tour (see Jan 12).
■ The *Empress of Australia*, which entered the Mersey flying the Yellow Jack, signifying a case of fever (smallpox) on board, disembarks its 4,000 passengers at Liverpool after they have each undergone a thorough 6hr medical examination.

20 Wednesday

New Zealand offers Britain a £1 million gift of **food**, including milk, dried eggs, cocoa, biscuits and tinned meat. It comes from the surplus allocation for US troops stationed in New Zealand.
■ A massive **explosion** and fire in the Monopol-Grimberg mine at Unna, nr Dortmund in the Ruhr. Nearly 500 miners and 3 British members of the Mines Inspectorate are trapped underground. 66 miners are

FEBRUARY

saved after rescue work directed by the British Military Government. All hope for the others is **abandoned** after the walls at the bottom of the shaft cave in. Only 16 bodies are recovered.
■ The **ballet** returns to Covent Garden with a performance of *The Sleeping Beauty*, with Margot Fonteyn as Princess Aurora, attended by the Royal Family.

21 Thursday

Police open fire on **mobs in Bombay** when they riot in support of the mutiny by the Royal Indian Navy men who are seeking better pay and accommodation, and quicker demobilisation.
■ With the slogan 'Dinners before diamonds', the lord mayor of Melbourne has asked for **jewellery** to auction for his Food for Britain appeal. The first gift is a diamond brooch worth £A500.
■ **Captain Edward Molyneux**, the famous British fashion designer, stages the first post-war fashion show in Paris.
. . . Denmark publishes a list of 2,671 acts of sabotage carried out by the Danish resistance against the occupying German forces . . .

22 Friday

An Ealing landlady who charged 30s. per week for a furnished room 12ft x 10ft, lit by candles and with the use of a kitchen, is ordered to **reduce the rent** to 15s. per week by magistrates.
■ The State Attorney in Oslo, Norway, has decided no action will be taken against Nobel prize-winning author **Knut Hamsun** (87) who engaged in propaganda for Germany during the occupation. Doctors have testified that Hamsun is suffering from seriously reduced mental power.
■ The French Constituent Assembly condemns the execution for murder and banditry of 20 Spanish Republicans, including two who fought with the French Resistance.

23 Saturday

Frank Sinatra is coming to Britain, paying his own fare, and for lower fees than he initially demanded, after many women said they would prefer to spend their money on dried eggs.
■ **Lt Gen Tomoyuki Yamashita**, former leader of the Japanese forces in the Philippines, is hanged nr Manila for war crimes. He was arraigned on 123 charges in connection with the many atrocities committed by troops under his command.
■ Karol Kurpanik, former commander of the **Auschwitz** concentration camp, is sentenced to death in Poland.
. . . SNOW falls in most parts of Scotland. Thurso has drifts 3-4ft deep . . .

24 Sunday

Aldershot's Military Detention Camp riot

CARTOON FUN . . . WITH RUGGLES

20

FEBRUARY

comes to an end when the 150 remaining army mutineers set fire to what remains of the former prison. The riot started on Saturday when 300 prisoners started throwing plates at each other. Half the prisoners surrendered and the rest continued the rampage.
■ **Gen Juan Peron** is elected president of Argentina. The governorship of all 14 provinces is won by Peron candidates and 26 out of 30 seats in the Senate.

25 Monday

The British steamship *Leeuwarden*, carrying 500 tons of potatoes, is **sunk by a mine** 18 miles north of Dieppe. The crew are taken safely to the port.
■ Hollywood film studio Metro-Goldwyn-Mayer is to show its films to wider audiences by sending out mobile projector units, known as **Metromobiles**, to isolated villages not served by cinemas. Soon the whole of rural Britain will be as familiar with the faces of Greer Garson, Clark Gable and Spencer Tracy as the town dwellers.
■ Crepe-soled sandals for children will be available this summer for the first time in 4yrs.
■ Automatic **announcements** linked with train indicator boards are to be introduced at Charing Cross, St James's Park and Waterloo stations on the District and Northern Lines of the London Underground, as an experiment, to leave the station staff free for other duties.

26 Tuesday

British troops in Palestine seize and question  5,000 Jews in their search for the terrorists who wrecked 22 RAF planes in Petah Tiqwa and Lydda last night.
■ **Princess Elizabeth**, (left) will take the salute at Sandhurst, for the first time, at the first passing out parade since the war.

27 Wednesday

Drastic cuts are made in food rations in the British Zone of Germany because of the world food shortage. The new rate of 1,014 calories per day for ordinary consumers is well below the 1,500 calories per day minimum considered essential by experts.
■ **Dancers** at London's Hammersmith Palais covered 126 million miles and wore ¾in. off the floorboards during the past 10yrs.
■ London's bus and train staff win a 2s. per week **pay rise** worth £1 million.
■ Roll-on **corsets** – not manufactured for 4yrs because of the rubber shortage – will be on sale in the spring for 5s.6d. and 7s.5d.

28 Thursday

Cheers greet the first consignment of **bananas** to appear in London's Spitalfields market.
■ Following the execution of Spanish republicans on February 22, the French government suspends all communication with Spain and warns of the danger to international peace and security of the dictatorial one-party Franco regime.
■ **Rickshaws** are to be abolished throughout China within the next 3yrs and replaced by buses and trams.

21

MARCH

MARCH

1 Friday
St David's Day

So popular have the Great Western Railway women announcers proved to be since their debut during the war, 40 are to remain on the staff. Some receive fan mail.
■ London's East End **tailors** are making winter coats for women and sports jackets for men out of ex-ARP blankets.

2 Saturday

Crime is on the increase in the USA. More serious crimes are reported in America than for 15yrs with a nation-wide daily average of 4,289.
■ The battleship HMS *Iron Duke*, Admiral Jellicoe's flagship at the battle of **Jutland** in World War I, has been sold for scrap.
■ **Chico Marx**, the mad pianist of the Marx Brothers team, wins £50,000 damages for repeated reference being made to him in a new film without his consent.
■ **Ho Chi Minh** is elected President of Communist Democratic Republic of North Vietnam *(see panel)*.
… Bali is liberated from the Japanese by the Dutch.

3 Sunday
New Moon

Two more **earthquakes** shake Switzerland, the most severe of a series since January 25 which have caused damage estimated at £223,000 so far.
■ Prime Minister **Clement Attlee** broadcasts to the nation appealing to both workers and employers to increase production.
■ While Devon, Cornwall and parts of Sussex bask in brilliant **sunshine**, most of SE England has an **Arctic** weekend with snowdrifts which in places top 20ft. Many districts are isolated by blizzards.

4 Monday

Dr Alan Nunn May, appears in court on spying charges *(see panel, facing page)*.
■ **Anti-British riots** in Alexandria, Egypt. Two British soldiers and 15 others are killed and 299 injured.
■ The first Housewives' Choice is broadcast on BBC radio. The first presenters are David Jacobs, Sam Costa, and Sam Heppner.

5 Tuesday

In a speech at Fulton, Missouri, **Winston Churchill** warns:

HO CHI MINH ON THE POWER TRAIL…

DATELINE: March 6
HO CHI MINH strides to power in VIETNAM, which becomes an autonomous state within French Indo-China. The French are the first major Western power to offcially recognize the Communist Democratic Republic. Ho Chi Minh, elected President on March 2, helped start the Communist Party in France in 1920. He led the resistance to the Japanese invasion and last year proclaimed independence.

MARCH

ATOM SECRETS MAN ARRESTED ON SPY CHARGES

MAR 4

THIS is the face of ALAN NUNN MAY, one of Britain's top scientists, arrested today and charged under the Official Secrets Act. During the war Dr May headed the Montreal Chalk River atomic project, and was recruited by Soviet intelligence. In 1944, they received from him a full report on atomic development in the USA, and samples of uranium 233 and 235, May received only $700 and two bottles of whisky for his espionage; he acted on the conviction that atomic energy should not be confined to the West.

'From Stettin in the Baltic to Trieste in the Adriatic an Iron Curtain has descended across the Continent.'
Mr Churchill urges Anglo-American 'fraternal association' to preserve peace.
■ The **Isle of Man** is stopping examinations for children passing from elementary school to secondary school to 'abolish snobbery'.
. . . Freezing temperatures all over Britain. 34°F in London . . .

6 Wednesday
Ash Wednesday

William Parker, a Los Angeles lecturer, has offered himself as a **human guinea pig** in the atomic bomb tests in the Pacific. He refuses to reveal his address for fear of being swamped by people who want his flat.
■ To help us cope in the food shortage, the Ministry of Food issues a recipe for **squirrel pie**.

7 Thursday

The **Nazi** state's debts, excluding reparations, amount to a staggering total of £20,000 million.
■ The British Medical Association is planning a £1½ million fund to fight what doesn't please them in the new **National Health Bill**, and is asking each of the country's 60,000 doctors to pledge £25.
■ **Charlie Chaplin** has a second son by his fourth wife, Oona O'Neill.

8 Friday

In the first **election** since 1937, Labour hold the London County Council, with 90 seats to the Conservatives 30. The Liberals and Communists have two seats each.

■ At the Oscars, **Joan Crawford** wins Best Actress for her performance in *Mildred Pierce,* and **Ray Milland** is Best Actor for *The Lost Weekend,* which also wins the Oscars for Best Picture and Best Director (Billy Wilder). For the first time, the Oscar-nominated songs are performed – by Kathryn Grayson, Dick Haymes, Dinah Shore and **Frank Sinatra** *(left).*
■ About a fifth of the total number of members of the new **Supreme Soviet** of the USSR are women.

23

MARCH

33 KILLED AS DISASTER STRIKES FA

MAR 9 — 33 spectators die and 500 are injured in the worst DISASTER in British football, at Bolton Wanderers' Burden Park stadium. The accident happens shortly after the start of Wanderers' FA Cup tie against Stoke City. Thousands of people break down fencing to get into the packed enclosure after police close the gates an hour before kick-off. In the panic that follows, the spectators already on the terraces lose their footing and are trampled. Others suffocate against the 3in steel crush-barriers. The FA launches an inquiry.

9 Saturday
Football's **Disaster Day**: 33 are killed at Bolton (*see panel*).

10 Sunday
The **Aga Khan**, spiritual leader of the Ismaili Moslems, is weighed in diamonds in Bombay. His 17 stone raises £550,000 for the welfare of the Ismaili community.

11 Monday
Queen Mary, accompanied by Princess Elizabeth, visits a factory in Herts where they are given samples of the factory's experimental product – nylon stockings. The stockings will soon be made in millions.

■ M Paul Spaak succeeds in forming a Socialist cabinet, and becomes Belgium's third premier since the liberation.

■ The ban on British ships using the **Panama Canal**, imposed last Sept to save dollars, is lifted.

■ Vera Lynn, the 'Forces Sweetheart', gives birth to a baby girl (*see panel, page 26*).

12 Tuesday
The police wage war on organised gangs specialising in **stealing new cars** for

MARCH

CUP TIE AT BOLTON

resale on the black market after 'camouflage factories' have changed them beyond recognition.
■ **Hams** cooked in the fire which destroyed the smokehouse of a meat shop in Kalamazoo, Michigan, USA, provide sandwiches for 100 firemen and spectators.
■ Film star **Judy Garland** and her producer husband Vincent Minelli, have a daughter, Liza *(picture, page 26)*.

13 Wednesday

Stalin *(pictured, above)*, in a reply to Winston Churchill's 'Iron Curtain' speech at Fulton, Missouri on Mar 5, says, 'Mr Churchill and his friends bear a close resemblance to Hitler and his friends. In fact, Mr Churchill has now adopted the position of war-monger.'
■ Thousands of women turn up in London looking for clothes **bargains** on the first day that they get better value for their clothing coupons.
■ An end is in sight to the lengthy negotiations on the future of **Indonesia**, though there is still fighting between the Dutch and the illegal Indonesian 'republic' government of Dr Soekarno. 'Republic' is thought to be a Japanese front.

14 Thursday

The people of New Zealand are ready to accept compulsory **food rationing** so that more can be sent to Britain.
■ Ted Stelle, head of music at a Hollywood radio station, has banned the broadcasting of **jive** because 'it is dirty or, at best, suggestive. The music itself is degenerate.'
■ Offers of work have poured in to **Gloria Vanderbilt** since she was cut off from her £5,000 p.a. income by her millionairess daughter Gloria Vanderbilt Stokowski. One US gramophone company said she could earn £75 a week by selling diamond-tipped needles.

15 Friday

Attlee offers India her **independence** from Britain.
■ Details of a secret process for manufacturing the **super-explosive** RDX were given to Russia by Canadian scientist Dr Raymond Boyer.
■ A total of 700 Arcon-type **prefabs** is being produced every week.

16 Saturday

Under a new Bill making **marriage** under the age of 16 illegal, girls of 12 and boys of

MARCH

YES, SIR – THAT'S MY BABY...

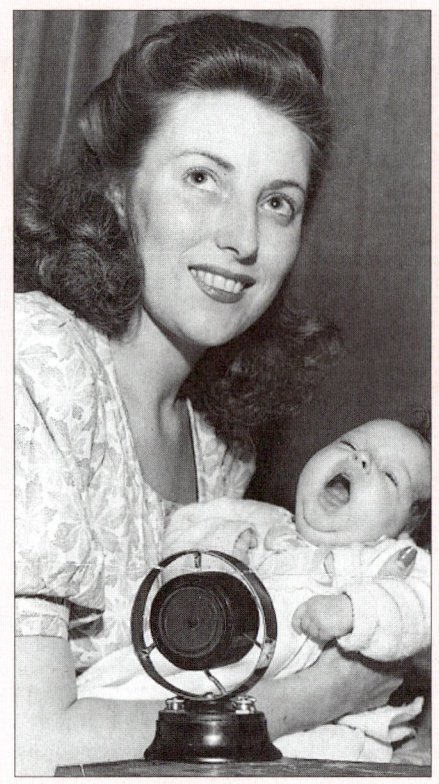

THERE'S a post-war baby boom, and among the stars with additions to the family are Forces' Sweetheart Vera Lynn (now Mrs Harry Lewis, *left*), with daughter Virginia; actress Judy Garland, with baby Liza, a daughter for her and husband Vincent Minelli (*centre*); and actor Stewart Granger (*right*), with his wife and new daughter, Lindsay. Charlie Chaplin and his fourth wife Oona O'Neill (not pictured) had a second son.

14 are no longer able to wed in Northern Ireland.
■ **Gunder Haegg** (Swe), champion miler and the holder of 7 world records, is banned from racing for life by the Swedish Amateur Athletics Association for accepting payments higher than those stipulated.

17 Sunday
Full Moon, St Patrick's Day

Italy is to hold a **referendum** and a general election on whether the country should retain the monarchy, and King
■ The 'Old Crocks', pre-1914 motor cycles, race from Tattenham Corner, Epsom, to Brighton, Sussex.
■ An area of 30 miles around the town of Luanhsien, China, has been rocked by earthquakes every day since September 30 last year, forcing the population to flee.

■ Police swoop on black market profiteers in Berlin and arrest more than 1,000 people.

18 Monday

French troops enter **Hanoi**, the capital of North Indo-China, taking over from the Chinese, who have had responsibility for N Indo-China since the Japanese surrender. They appeal to the people to stay calm.
■ Making its bow in Coventry is a permanent **theatre** company of young players, called the Arts Midland Theatre Co, under the director/producer and distinguished actress Beatrix Lehmann.

19 Tuesday

Princess Elizabeth launches the biggest aircraft carrier ever built in Britain, HMS *Eagle* (*left*) at the Harland & Wolff shipyard in Belfast. It's the 20th Royal Navy ship of this name, and is the successor to the aircraft carrier which went down

escorting the Malta convoy in August, 1942.
■ The French government is to hold a **referendum** on its proposed new constitution on May 5 and will call a general election on June 2.
■ Theo Medina (FR), fighting **Jackie Paterson** (GB) in the European Bantamweight Championship at the Albert Hall, London, is disqualified for a low blow and Paterson becomes the new champion, despite being floored 3 times.

20 Wednesday

The government announces that women may now become **diplomats** – so long as they do not marry.
■ Oxford and Cambridge colleges, as well as several English cathedrals and churches, are making gifts towards the restoration of the **Monte Cassino** library, Italy. It's thought that the 1,250 manuscripts in the library were removed to safety before the abbey was destroyed in the Allied onslaught.
■ Thousands of **women fight**, scream and scratch in Times Square, New York, USA, when paper stockings, which can be exchanged for nylons, are dropped from a plane.

21 Thursday

The Minister of Health, **Aneurin Bevan**, presents the National Health Service Bill to Parliament.
■ Britain's number one film star, **James Mason** (*right*) who is currently filming *Odd Man Out*, is to make his home in Hollywood. He will move there in September.
■ At the Nazi war crimes trials in Nuremburg, **Goering** denies that either he or Hitler knew anything about 'the Final Solution'.

22 Friday

A treaty of friendship and alliance is signed by Britain and **Transjordan**, at the same time as Transjordan is recognised as an independent state.
■ The medical journal *The Lancet* urges doctors to drop all-out opposition to the National Health Bill.
. . . Two people are killed and 100 are injured in a day-long FOOD RIOT in Messina, Italy . . .

23 Saturday

It is reported from Naples, Italy, where he has lived since being deported from New York, that the infamous gangster **Charles 'Lucky' Luciano** is planning to write a book about the New York underworld.
■ An international **crime-fighting** centre has been established by the Dutch government in consultation with Scotland Yard at the Hague.

24 Sunday

The **Overseas Service** of the BBC begins broadcasts in Russian.
■ The famous Spanish cellist, **Pablo Casals**, cancels his English tour, 'to avoid playing in a country that recognises Franco's government'.
■ **Mary Pickford**, 'America's sweetheart' of the silent screen and former wife of Douglas Fairbanks, arrives on her first visit to Britain since 1939.
. . . Thick FOG blankets the English Channel . . .

25 Monday

Formal opening of **Heathrow Airport** by Lord Winster, Minister of Civil Aviation. Because Heathrow is very difficult for foreigners to say, it is to be called London Airport. It is to be enlarged so it can handle up to 160 aircraft per hour.
■ A 7hr-day for **cab horses** with a 1hr break for rest, food and drink, is decreed by Windsor Corporation, Berks.

MARCH

MARCH

Taking to the Skies in 1946

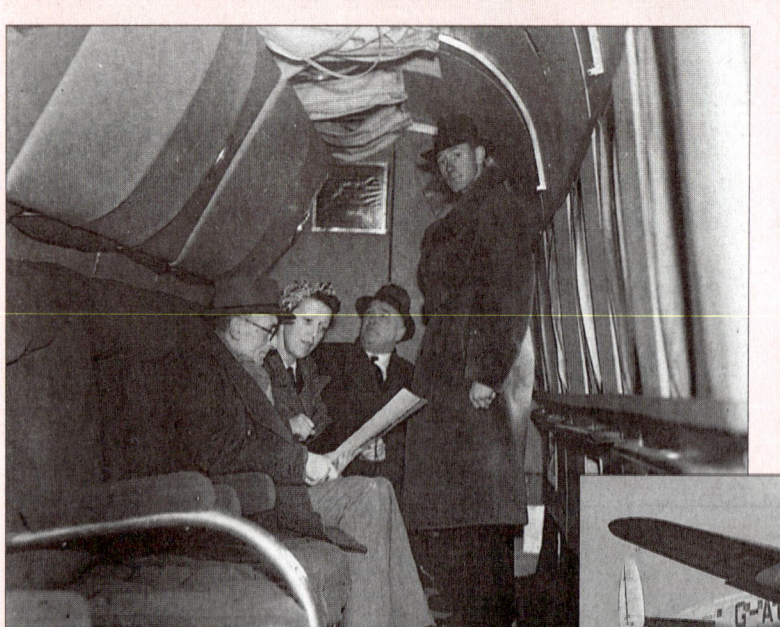

Aircraft design, revolutionised by the needs of war, is undergoing further radical change. In Bristol, the world's biggest aircraft hangar, covering 35,000 sq ft, is built for the construction of the giant 244-seater *Brabazon (above)*. **The move from war to peace is illustrated by the** *Lancastrian (below),* **which is quickly and cheaply converted from a Lancaster bomber to carry passengers up to 4,000 miles at a top speed of 310 mph. Faster speeds are accomplished by the new jet aircraft such as the De Havilland Vampire and the Gloster Meteor.**

Familiar sights in our skies: (Facing page clockwise from top): The De Havilland Swallow; Mosquito; Gloster Meteor; Sunderland Flying Boat; and (above) the De Havilland Vampire.

MARCH

OK, So which one is the Spitfire?

Can you tell them apart? They were two key weapons that saw Fighter Command through the dark days of the battle of Britain to the end of the war . . . identify the Hurricane and the Spitfire pictured, left.
Answer on page 96.

29

MARCH

26 Tuesday

Winston Churchill returns to England on the *Queen Mary* from his holiday in the USA.
■ The **biggest aircraft hanger** in the world, covering 35,000 square feet, is being built at Filton nr Bristol (see page 28).
■ London's 30,000 caterers are to be given special concessions to provide food and drink for the millions of people who will be pouring into London for the **Victory Parade** and celebrations on June 8.

27 Wednesday

Soviet Foreign Secretary **Andrei Gromyko** walks out of the UN Security Council meeting when it rejects a Russian motion that the debate on Persia's appeal to the UN about the continued presence of Russian troops on its soil should be postponed.
■ Twenty-three **VCs**, 685 DSOs, and 14,640 other awards were won by the Royal Navy, the Royal Marines and the Dominion Navies in World War II.
■ A cheque for £80,000 is presented to the Red Cross and St John (the wartime coalition of the Red Cross and the Knights Hospitallers) by the War Office. The money has been collected by ex-prisoners of war in Germany who received Red Cross parcels while in captivity.

28 Thursday

Free milk in schools (⅓ pint per child per day), will begin with the payment of family allowances in August, and free school dinners will be provided at the earliest possible date by all grant-aided primary and secondary schools. Dinners will have to wait until school canteen facilities can meet the expected demand.
■ **Mr Averell Harriman**, *left*, is to be the new US ambassador at the Court of St James. He originally came to London in 1940 to expedite the Lend Lease arrangements, and was US Ambassador to the USSR from 1945 until now.
■ Seven people are killed and 6 are missing when a **Sunderland** flying-boat crashes on take-off in Sunderland.

29 Friday

The **Gold Coast** becomes the first British Colony with majority black rule.
■ **Holiday-makers** are advised to take soap and sweets away with them – there will be no extra allocation of soap and only a slightly increased sweet ration in holiday spots.
■ **Rocky Graziano** (USA, *above*, pictured during a later defence against Tony Zale), becomes the new World welterweight champion, knocking out Marty Servo (USA) in the 2nd round of their fight in New York.
■ The parents of **Violet Szabo**, one of the British Special Operations executives who operated in France during the war, receive official confirmation of their daughter's death in Ravensbruck concentraion camp.

30 Saturday

The TUC call on women to go back to the factories so that Britain can secure and maintain a high standard of living.
■ The cruiser *Montcalm* brings back to France 225 tons of **gold** sent to Martinique for safe-keeping in 1940.
■ Brilliant **sunshine** and temperatures in the 70s bring out the motorists, who use their precious petrol ration for a trip to the seaside where thousands bask on the packed beaches.

31 Sunday

The Duke of Gloucester is 46 today.
■ **Fiorello La Guardia**, ex-Mayor of New York, is elected Director-General of UNRRA (the United Nations Relief and Rehabilitation Administration).

APRIL

DARK BLUES STORM TO BOAT RACE TRIUMPH

Oxford beats Cambridge in the 92nd Boat Race (the first to be held for 6yrs) by three lengths in 19min 54sec. *The winning Oxford line-up (above, from left): Cox R Ebsworth-Snow; R Bourne; P Brodie, J Cleave, J Carstairs, G Robertson-Campbell, D Jamison; R Turner-Warwick; R Raikes and reserve man A Purssell, pictured in training at Henley.*

■ The first election to be held in **Greece** since 1935 is won by pro-royalist parties.

■ **Russia** becomes the first UN member to pay its full contribution to the UN's working capital, which dispels rumours that the Russians might quit the organization after Gromyko walked out of the security council meeting on March 27.

1 APRIL
Monday

Elastic snaps back into production.

■ The **Means Test** for people at present on the unemployment register and likely to remain jobless for some time will be abolished on April 8.

■ An **earthquake** on the Pacific seabed in the Aleutian trench generates a seismic wave that destroys Scotch Cap lighthouse (14m above sea level), on Unimak Island, and reaches Hawaii 5hrs later, killing 300 people. It then sweeps on to Alaska and the west coast of America.

APRIL

2 Tuesday

Seventeen MPs table a motion protesting against MPs who write **anonymous** articles criticising their fellows, saying, 'it's contrary to the decent and friendly traditions of this House'.
■ Traffic experts are to study Derby Day for hints on how to control the traffic in London on **V-Day** (June 8).
... London fashion designers show glamorous garments in SILKS, crepes and satin, in an effort to pep up wardrobes this summer ...

3 Wednesday

A committee recommends that the UK should stage a big international **exhibition** in Britain in 1951.
■ Workers in the **National Savings** Movement from all over Britain have been invited to a Garden Party to be given by the King at Buckingham Palace on June 4.
■ Lt General Masaharu Homma, the infamous supreme commander of the Japanese Forces in the Philippines and accused of responsibility for the Bataan death march, is **executed** in Manila for war crimes .
... It is the hottest April 3 for 90yrs. The temperature is 75°F at Kew ...

4 Thursday

World hunger increases. India needs 4,000,000 tons of rice for the rest of the year. She can't import pre-war levels of rice from Burma. The world wheat deficit is now 8,000,000 tons. In France the bread ration is down to 300gms per person per day. Holland will have no bread from the middle of August until harvest in October, and it will be years before land flooded by salt water will be fertile. Italy has no grain stocks, and in Poland a complete lack of bread is threatened within a month.
... Temperature in London reaches 79° F ...

5 Friday

Mr J Morant's **Lovely Cottage** (left,)ridden by Capt R Petre, wins the first Grand National since 1940.
■ **Queens Park Rangers** football club have searched everywhere for football **boots**, either new or secondhand for their players. They are now appealing to anyone who can spare a pair in sizes 6, 7 or 8.
... Air letters from London to Buenos Aires, Argentina, are now delivered in 2 days ...

6 Saturday

The white charger on which General **Rommel** boasted he would ride in triumph through Cairo and which was later given to Field Marshal Montgomery, arrives at Tilbury Docks from Germany. It may take part in the Victory Day parade.
■ Half a million temporary **civil servants** on Grades 1, 2 and 3 are to receive pay increases of 3s. per week for men and 2s.6d.

LARRY REIGNS SUPREME IN ROLE AS HENRY V

Laurence Olivier's new film *Henry V* opens to wide acclaim in the United States. *Time* magazine is fulsome in its praise, declaring it 'a masterpiece'.

APRIL

for women, backdated to January 1.
■ The annual performance of Bach's St Matthew Passion is given by the Bach Choir at Southwark Cathedral today and at the Albert Hall tomorrow.

7 Sunday

Whenever the Rev W J Hamilton of Pasadena, California, calls out **'Amen'** to his congregation, he gets a chorus of motor-car horns in response. He preaches every Sunday to 1,500 motorists who drive into a tree-ringed enclosure and remain in their cars throughout the service. 'I'm hoping this "park and pray" movement will spread throughout the country,' he says.
... The Iranian government reveals that the USSR is to get 51% control of Iranian OIL for 25yrs ...

8 Monday

Between 10-12 million books, as well as great numbers of manuscripts, were lost by fire in the **blitz**. The most serious losses are in educational, scientific and historical works, which will be reprinted asap. It will take about 7yrs to make good the losses.
■ **J Arthur Rank** meets some of Britain's top women film stars at his newly acquired **Pinewood Studios**, which have just been freed by the government. Among those present are Jean Simmons, Patricia Roc, Valerie Hobson, Jean Kent and Sally Gray.
■ **W Somerset Maugham** has given the manuscript of his book Of Human Bondage to the US Library of Congress in Washington as a token of Anglo-American friendship.

9 Tuesday

The **BBC** television service from Alexandra Palace, which was suspended at the beginning of the war, will start again on June 7. Programmes will be broadcast daily from 3.00pm-4.30pm and 8.30pm-10.00pm.
■ In the **Budget**, Chancellor of the Exchequer **Hugh Dalton** (left) announces that personal allowances will be raised from £80-£110 p.a. for a single person and from £140-£180 p.a. for married couples; workers' NI contributions will be tax-free, and purchase tax will be abolished on a wide range of items, from glass and plastic articles used to preserve or serve food to utility mattresses, kitchen cupboards, electric kettles, typewriters, thermal insulation covers for domestic water heaters and public clocks. Tax will also be reduced from 100% to 33½% on wooden walking sticks, hair waving and drying machines, cameras and enlargers, musical instruments including gramophones, and gramophone records.

10 Wednesday

Over 4,000 people have signed a petition asking the National Gallery, London, to continue with its programme of **lunchtime concerts**, which it ran so successfully during the War.
■ Policewomen are to be allowed to marry and keep their jobs.
... All brothels in France must close – by decree of the French parliament ...
■ The Liberals win the General election in **Japan**. It is the first to give the vote to women and young men, and is under the direct supervision of the Allied occupation forces. About a third of the voters were women.

11 Thursday

The **World's Fair** site at Flushing Meadow, Long Island, about 10 miles from New York City, is to be the temporary headquarters of the United Nations.
■ Britain's **jam ration** is to be doubled for a month, from May 26-June 26, to 2lbs a book.
■ From May 6, any woman of any nationality,

APRIL

except German, may come to Britain for domestic employment.

12 Friday

The **Royal Observatory** is to move from Greenwich to Hurstmonceux Castle, Sussex, (*above*) because of the poor light and atmospheric pollution in London.
■ Two hours **free beauty treatment** every fortnight in the firm's time and a free permanent wave every 3 months is offered by a New Zealand corset-making company to persuade girls to work there. Competition for female labour is so keen that New Zealand is calling itself 'Eve's Paradise'.

13 Saturday

Doctors all over the country are working overtime to cope with two minor illnesses - gastric 'flu and 'spring fatigue'. The unseasonal warm weather is blamed.
■ The 34,000 ton battleship HMS *Nelson* is being turned into a training ship for the Home Fleet. It will have accommodation for 400 trainees.
■ Film star **Jean Kent** (*right*) marries businessman Yusef Rouart at St George's, Hanover Square. Actor **Stewart Granger** is best man.

14 Saturday

British Summer Time begins

A chewed-looking **letter** received in Bristol bears on the envelope a postman's writing: 'eaten by snails in letter box'.
■ Many different RAF and naval aircraft, including Lancasters, Meteors, Mosquitoes, Spitfires, Hurricanes, Wellingtons, Firebrands and Sea Mosquitoes (*pictures page 28*), which became famous during the war, will fly over London in squadron formation as part of the **Victory Parade** on June 8.

15 Monday

The 'king's shilling' has gone up to £25 tax free, in an effort to attract men into the forces.
■ **Princess Margaret** is confirmed at Windsor Castle by the Archbishop of Canterbury in the presence of the King, the Queen, Princess Elizabeth and Queen Mary.
■ Police had to be called to organise the queues 2hrs before a store in Morecambe, Lancs, opened. 3,000 women had turned up to buy fully fashioned silk stockings at 3s.11d. a pair.
■ The **Golden Arrow**, the daily passenger service from London to Paris, comes back into service on Southern Railways. It leaves Victoria Station each morning at 10am.

16 Tuesday
Full Moon

Penicillin treatment is being given at Aix-les-Bains, the fashionable French spa near Geneva.
■ The **Eureka Diamond** – the first ever found in South Africa, and now the centrepiece of a bracelet - is sold in London for £5,700.
. . . Miners will get the day off on V-Day, June 8, and £1 bonus . . .

17 Wednesday

The government announce plans to **nationalise** the iron and steel industries.
■ Police in Rome arrest 3 women and 11 men who are running a **begging racket**. They employ 200 children to prey on the sympathies of soldiers.

34

APRIL

18 Thursday

The **League of Nations** in Geneva is formally dissolved.
■ British ATS girls in **Palestine** begin the formidable task of sorting more than 1,000 bags of mail piled up in Jerusalem's strike-bound post office. Addresses in Hebrew and Arabic are their biggest headache.
■ The new Greek Monarchist government **resigns** after only 2 weeks in office.

19 Friday
Good Friday

The US government orders a 25% cut in the consumption of **flour** to meet what President Truman has described as history's greatest threat of mass starvation. He promises a million tons of wheat a month for Europe and Asia.
. . . The French Assembly adopts the new Constitution for the Fourth Republic by 309 votes to 249 . . .

20 Saturday

The winner of the British Marbles Championship held at Tinsley Green, Sussex, is Harry Longridge of Crawley, Sussex, who played **marbles** today for the first time since he left school.
■ More city people than ever are keeping **pigs**, according to the Small Pig Keepers' Council. A Ministry of Agriculture spokesman says that 'many men out of the Forces want to keep pigs, but we discourage them because of the shortage of pig food.'

21 Sunday

Princess Elizabeth is 20 today. Nearly 40,000 people pack the grounds of Windsor Castle hoping to see Princess Elizabeth and the rest of the royal family, who are staying at the castle. Women faint, and families lose one another in the crush.

DATELINE: April 21 JOHN MAYNARD KEYNES (63), the influential economist, dies. The originator of the Keynsian theory of economics, he was leader of the British delegation to the Bretton Woods Conference of 1944 and played an influential part in the setting up of the International Monetary Fund.

---

22 Monday
Easter Monday

Attendance at outdoor events this **Bank Holiday** breaks all records. 43 football matches are watched by 707,000 people; Whipsnade Zoo has 18,000 visitors, and 70,000 people queue for 3hrs to visit London Zoo. Hampstead Heath Fair reports takings of £1,000 an hour.
■ Prisoners in San Vittore Gaol, Milan, Italy, riot. Tanks and troops surround the prison and behind this cordon, relatives wait with suitcases full of clothes in case the prisoners get through.

23 Tuesday
St George's Day

Unknown people, thought to be Fascists, have dug up and removed Mussolini's body from its unmarked grave in the Maggiore Cemetry in Milan, Italy.
■ Some of the 300,000 Jewish and Arab civil servants on strike in Jerusalem smash chairs and tables and throw them at their strike committee when it orders them to end the strike.
■ Air Vice Marshal D C T Bennett, piloting a British Airways Star Light, sets a **new record** for the flight from London to Buenos Aires, Argentina, of 29hr 5min.

24 Wednesday

Stevenage, Herts, is scheduled to be the first New Town in Britain. It will cost more than £19 million to build everything from homes to pram parks for 50,000 people.
■ Miss Mary Hollowell (33), a solicitor from Needham Market, nr Ipswich, Suffolk, is appointed the first woman coroner in England.
■ The 2,500 rebellious **prisoners** in San Vittore Gaol, Milan *(see April 22)*, hoist a white flag and open the prison doors following the threat of an artillery assault.

APRIL

6 convicts were killed and 4 wounded in the disturbances.

25 Thursday

The **Big Four** (USA, USSR, UK and France) foreign ministers meet in Paris. The Russians, led by Mr Molotov, are demanding heavy reparations from Italy.
■ A national ballot of nearly 600,000 people vote James Mason and **Margaret Lockwood** (right) the most popular British film stars and *The Way to the Stars* the best British film made between 1939-1945.
■ The **British loaf** is reduced in size by 4oz, and brewing is cut by 15% to save grain.

26 Friday

The Trades Union Congress want to see a 40hr working week, but its implementation by easy stages.
■ The French Assembly approves the nationalisation of French **coalmines**.
■ **The King** has his first racing win of the season when his horse *Golden Coach* scores an easy victory at Litchfield Park.
■ Nearly 1,500 **Jews** are questioned, and 69 are held in custody, in Tel Aviv as both the British and Jewish authorities condemn the murder of 7 British soldiers in a **terrorist raid** on the border of Tel Aviv and Jaffa on the 24th.

27 Saturday

The **King and Queen**, accompanied by Princess Elizabeth, join a crowd of 98,000 at Wembley to see **Derby County** beat Charlton Athletic 4-1 in the FA Cup Final, at Wembley (right).
■ **Sir Lewis Casson**, actor and a vice-president of Equity, the actors' union, says that Westminster Theatre is 'lost to the profession', having been bought for £132,500 for the staging of Moral Rearmament plays.
. . . Henry Cotton (GB) wins *The Star* golf tournament at Wentworth, Surrey.

28 Sunday

The Old Vic Company, led by **Laurence Olivier** and **Vivien Leigh**, fly to New York for a 6-week season.
■ Film technicians at a conference in London severely criticize film producer Gabriel Pascal for what they consider a waste of time, money and materials in his £1.3million film production of *Caesar and Cleopatra*.
. . . **New York's latest attempt to glamorize girls who wear glasses are spectacle frames studded with jewels** . . .

29 Monday

The **Citizen's Advice Bureaux**, which have dealt with more than 1 million problems since they were set up the day after the war broke out, are here to stay.
■ Food permits will be issued to organisers of public parties on **Victory Day** (June 8).

APRIL

BRITAIN IN THE GRIP OF FOOD RATIONING

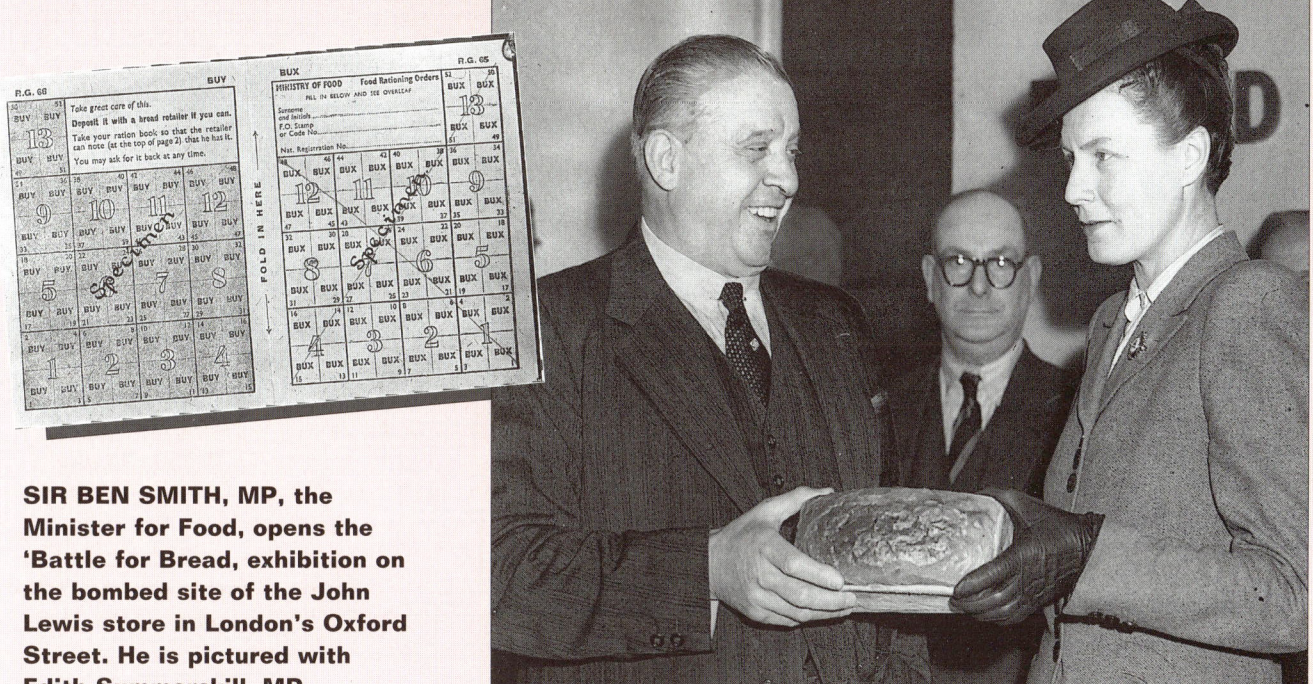

SIR BEN SMITH, MP, the Minister for Food, opens the 'Battle for Bread, exhibition on the bombed site of the John Lewis store in London's Oxford Street. He is pictured with Edith Summerskill, MP, examining one of the new economy loaves. Throughout 1946, food shortages are acute and many staple items are rationed Pictured below (left) is a typical week's ration for one person. The Dominions and the USA are among the many countries cutting back on their own food supplies in order to help Europe's increasingly hungry population. The queue (below right) is for bread coupons, when bread is rationed for the first time in the UK.

37

APRIL

WHAT'S ON AT THE THEATRE

The theatre belongs to the actors rather than the dramatists in 1946. Audiences are so keen to go to the theatre, there is no need for producers to find new plays of high calibre: a notable exception is *The Winslow Boy*, starring Emlyn Williams. The acting is of a quality seldom surpassed in the history of theatre. The work of three men stands out – Laurence Olivier, Ralph Richardson and John Gielgud.

Pictured: (Left to right) Alec Guinness, one of the few actors who makes up from a palette; The hit play The Winslow Boy; Ralph Richardson and Margaret Leighton, who star in Cyrano de Bergerac.

CRIME AND PUNISHMENT	John Gielgud, Peter Ustinov, Edith Evans
KING LEAR	Laurence Olivier, Alec Guinness, Pamela Brown, Margaret Leighton
AN INSPECTOR CALLS	Ralph Richardson, Alec Guinness, Margaret Leighton
CYRANO DE BERGERAC	Ralph Richardson, Alec Guinness, Margaret Leighton
THE WINSLOW BOY	Emlyn Williams, Clive Morton, Angela Baddeley, Kathleen Harrison
MUCH ADO ABOUT NOTHING	Robert Donat, Renee Ascherson
THE KING MAKER	John Clements, Robert Eddison, Kay Hammond
ANTONY AND CLEOPATRA	Godfrey Tearle, Edith Evans
GRAND NATIONAL NIGHT	Leslie Banks, Charles Groves, Hermione Baddeley

They will provide not more than one tea meal and two hot beverages per person. The allocations per person are: margarine ¼oz; sugar (per meal) ⅛oz; sugar (per hot beverage) ⅛oz; preserves ⅛oz; tea 1lb for 225 hot beverages; milk 9 pints per 100 hot beverages.

■ The trial of **General Hideki Tojo**, Prime Minister of Japan at the time of the massive air attack on Pearl Harbour that brought America into the war, begins in Tokyo.

30 Tuesday

MPs are to receive a pay rise. Their salaries will be increased by £400 p.a. to £1,000 p.a.

■ As there has been so little sunshine this season, army **searchlights** are being used to dry part of Australia's vine fruit crop. And anglers in Sydney, where there is a black market in fish bait are charged 8d. a worm.

■ The **Big Four** meeting in Paris *(see April 25)* rules out the return of the South Tyrol to Austria.

MAY

1 Wednesday
New Moon

Penicillin will be in the shops in June and available to anyone on a doctor's prescription.
■ Disgraced atomic scientist **Alan Nunn May** is sentenced to 10yrs penal servitude for betraying secrets to the Russians.

■ The Anglo-American report on **Palestine** recommends that 100,000 immigrants should be authorized immediately and Palestine should be neither a Jewish nor an Arab state. Prime Minister **Attlee** asks to what extent the US government would share the military and financial responsibility for this, and that both Jewish and Arab armies are disbanded.
■ Chancellor of the Exchequer **Hugh Dalton** succeeds Lord Keynes as Governor of the International Monetary Fund and Bank of Reconstruction and Recovery.

2 Thursday

Actress **Winifred Shotter**, and **Jasmine Bligh**, who was a radio announcer during the war, are to share the job of the BBC woman TV announcer.
■ Rum – nearly 4 million gallons of it – leaves Kingston, Jamaica on a ship bound for the UK.
■ Britain acts to help the **hungry** people of the world with more cuts at home and the loan of 50,000 tons of wheat to Italy.
■ Tall girls in the USA are congratulating 6ft 3in actress **Dorothy Ford** on getting the lead in a new **Mickey Rooney** film in Hollywood. 'It's hard for a tall girl to find romance,' says one.

3 Friday

Arabs stone British troops in Jerusalem in protest against the Anglo-American plan for **Palestine** which recommends that the British mandate should continue until 'Arab-Jewish hostility disappears'.
■ The King's horse *Hypericum*, ridden by D Smith, wins the 1,000 Guineas at Newmarket by a length and a half.
■ *The Daily Mail* is 50 today (first issue 1896). At a celebration dinner at the Dorchester Hotel, London, **Lord Rothermere** presides over a company of 500 distinguished guests. A message of congratulation from the King is read out, and **Winston Churchill** (Leader of the Opposition, *right*) proposes the toast.

MAY

4 Saturday

The **Football** Players' Union accepts 'under protest' the Football League's offer to professional footballers of a £10 weekly wage in the playing season and £7.10s. in the close season.

■ The secret Jewish radio 'Voice of Israel' promises that the **Jewish underground** will observe law and order if 100,000 Jews are admitted to Palestine, but the groups refuse to give up their arms, as demanded by Mr Attlee.

5 Sunday

Thousands of **film fans** travel to the 12th century Linchmere Church, Haslemere, Surrey, to see **Stewart Granger**'s daughter, Lindsay, christened in the presence of many leading lights of the British film industry. Granger, his wife, actress Elspeth March, and their guests are mobbed (above).

■ Two pure Arab chestnut horses are on their way to England as presents for Princess Elizabeth and Princess Margaret from the Emir Abdullah of Transjordan.

■ **Civil War** in China as fighting breaks out between the Communists and the Nationalists on the Yangtse river.

6 Monday

The Air Ministry now offers a new official service – long-range **weather forecasts** for holiday-makers and important outdoor events such as the Derby.

■ About 25 German scientists, all non-Nazis, many of whom are aeronautical authorities, are coming to Britain to work with British scientists at Farnborough on solving the aerodynamic and metallurgic problems created by **jet engines**.

■ The Society of Registered Male Nurses is offering a prize for the best list of titles for men in nursing - from student nurse to matron.

7 Tuesday

There is **uproar** in the House of Commons when Prime Minister Clement Attlee announces the withdrawal of British troops from Egypt, depending on effective

ZOO'S NEW STAR

THOUSANDS queue at London Zoo this month to see Lien Ho, the zoo's new panda. It is a gift from China.

MAY

arrangements being made for the defence of the Suez Canal.
■ The French Cabinet meets to consider the country's rejection of a proposed one-chamber constitution by 10,450,000 votes to 9,289,386.
■ **Cecilia Colledge** (25) regains her title as Britain's champion woman figure-skater.
. . . Anton Mussert, whom Hitler named the 'Fuhrer' of the Netherlands, is executed for war crimes at the Hague, Holland . . .

8 Wednesday

The Government is proposing to create 20 **new towns** to house one million people at a cost of £380 million.
■ Film star **Madeleine Carroll** is granted a divorce from her husband actor **Sterling Hayden**. When asked if he was going to marry again, Hayden replied, 'Believe me, brother, no'.
The maximum retail price of new potatoes is fixed at 4½d a lb until June 10.

9 Thursday

Victor Emmanuel III of Italy abdicates. He is succeeded by **King Umberto II** (left).
■ **Farmworkers** accept the offer of a minimum wage of £4, but are to continue fighting for £4.10s.
■ **Winston Churchill** claims his place in Dutch history by becoming the first foreigner to address the States General in the Hague.
. . . The Post Office announces that Victory stamps will go on sale on June 11 . . .

10 Friday

The US Senate approves a £937 million **loan** to Britain by 46 votes to 34, after 3 weeks of debate. The Bill now goes before the House of Representatives.
■ Because of the **emancipation** of women, a husband is no longer bound by law to pay for his wife's funeral if she has set nothing aside for it in her will.
■ In Paris the **Big Four** agree on placing Italy's former colonies in North Africa under UN control.

11 Saturday

The Attorney General, **Sir Hartley Shawcross** (right) appoints 35 legal teams to deal with nearly 50,000 service divorces still waiting to be heard.
■ Some star victims of the Hollywood housing shortage are living in their dressing rooms, among them **Victor Mature**.
■ The first post-war **Leipzig Fair** opens in the Russian zone of occupied Germany. Items on view include miniature cameras at £10 each, portable typewriters for £12 each and a new model 6-cylinder 40hp car for £187.

12 Sunday

Mr C Harvey of Maristow, Devon, has a **clock** that tells the date, the day, the month, the moon and the tides – and rings a bell when dinner is cooked.
■ A BOAC **flying boat** takes off from Poole, Dorset to re-open the 12,000 mile Empire Route to Australia, suspended during the war.
■ On his arrival in Washington for talks on the world food crisis, **Herbert Morrison**, Lord President of the Council, says that famine will soon be killing more civilians and turning out future fascists more quickly than Hitler or Mussolini ever managed.

13 Monday

A **41-gun salute** in London's Hyde Park marks the 9th anniversary of the King's Coronation.
■ The BBC appoints **McDonald Hobley** as its male TV announcer.
■ The King gives £300 to the appeal to

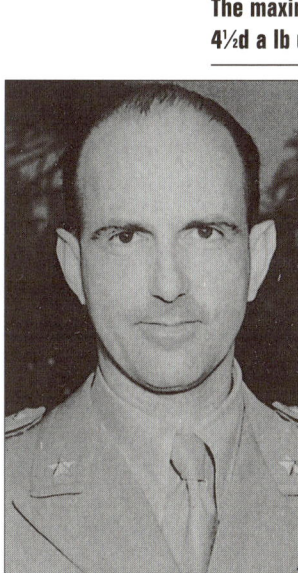

41

MAY

14 Tuesday

reconstruct Coventry Cathedral, which was almost totally destroyed during the Blitz.
. . . **The price of the AUSTIN 8 is to be increased by £15 to £345.15s** . . .

500 women in Ascoli, Italy, storm a bakery and seize 300lbs of bread.
■ 2,000 Japanese stage a **sit-down strike** outside the gates of the Imperial Palace in Tokyo, demanding food.
■ British light-heavyweight boxing champion **Freddie Mills** is knocked out of the world title fight in the 10th round by Gus Lesnevich (USA) at Harringay Arena, London *(see panel, above)*.
■ Hard knocks for farmers – there's snow in Yorkshire, a drought in the Lake District, hail in Snowdonia, and frost and cold winds in Lincolnshire.

15 Wednesday

A programme calling for equal rights for women in all fields has been laid before the UN Commission on **Human Rights** in New York.
■ There is a plague of **locusts**, 'unprecedented in history', in Sardinia. It will be fought with British pesticide which 5 aircraft, hired for £200 an hour, will carry from Bovingdon, Herts.
■ 1,800 illegal Jewish immigrants on the Rumanian ship *Smyrna*, are captured by British destroyers and escorted into Haifa.

MAY

THE RING MASTERS OF 1946

JOE LOUIS is back. Heavyweight champion of the world since 1937, Louis returns to the ring after service in the US Army as a PT instructor. He has been boosting morale by undertaking exhibition bouts. Despite having put on some weight and shed some hair, Louis *(centre, left)* comes back to knock out his old adversary Billy Conn (USA) in the 8th round. *Far left:* **Rocky Graziano (USA)** becomes world welterweight champion, knocking out his compatriot, Matty Servo, in the 2nd round of their fight in New York.
Left: **Freddie Mills**, the British light-heavyweight champion, who is knocked in the 10th round of his world title tilt by Gus Lesnevich (USA) at Harringay Arena, London. *Right (top):* **Louis** delivers the haymaker that stops Conn; *(bottom)* Britain's **Bruce Woodcock** *(right)* on his way to an 8th-round victory over Lesnevich.

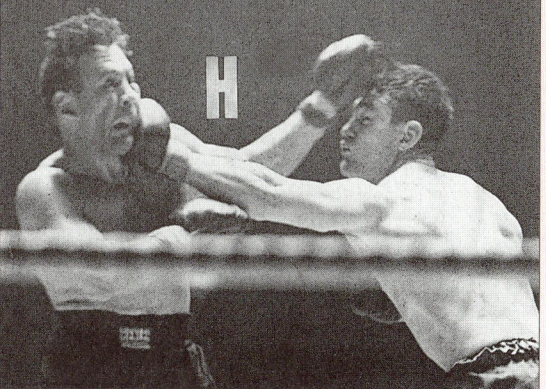

LOUIS RETURNS TO SHOW HE'S LOST NONE OF HIS OLD POWER

16 Thursday
Full Moon

Prime Minister Attlee reveals the plans for an independent **united India**.

■ 4,000 men and 1,000 women will be on duty for the St John Ambulance Brigade on **V-Day** – all without pay.

■ Twenty-eight passenger **gliders**, built for the RAF at a cost of several hundred pounds each are being sold, minus wings, for £5 each at Wolverhampton Aerodrome.

17 Friday

60,000 new **telephones** are being installed in Britain every month.

. . . **France nationalizes its coal mines** . . .

■ Tucks and frills are the main features of the first non-austerity blouses and skirts coming this autumn. Some of the day-wear blouses sport gold and silver sequin epaulets, and skirts have plenty of swinging pleats.

■ A 6-week **drought** in the Lake District ends with freak storms – thunder and lightning mixed with snow, hail and torrential rain.

18 Saturday

The census in **Japan** reveals that the population is 73,110,995.

■ Edward James of Chicago, one of the wealthiest negroes in the USA, pays £125,000 ransom after being **kidnapped** by masked gunmen.

. . . **Violent rain in England, drought in Scotland** . . .

43

MAY

19 Sunday

British film actress **Peggy Cummins**, 20, (left) is sacked from the film *Forever Amber*, because the film's producer Darryl F Zanuck thinks that in the early shots she looks no older than 13. But he predicts that she is headed for Hollywood stardom.
- The King's **Victory Day** greeting is printed on 6,875,000 cards for distribution to schoolchildren.

20 Monday

The Minister of Education announces that any student who has won an award other than a State scholarship or local authority major award to university, but is unable to take it up because of economic hardship, will be eligible for a **maintenance grant**.
- 11 million shell eggs, 67 tons of dried eggs and 1,530 tons of bacon arrive at Liverpool from Canada.

21 Tuesday

Gold coins worth £125,000 – the money with which the Nazis intended to finance their last stand in Bavaria – has been discovered in Salzburg.
- As aids to tastier meals, more meat products including jellied veal and pork, stewing steak and meat puddings will be on sale from today until June 12.

22 Wednesday

The Dominion Premiers Conference opens in London.
- The US State Department says that the immediate transfer of 100,000 Jews to **Palestine** stands as the official US government policy.
- Orders for 100,000 gross eye-lash curlers are received by a firm showing at the Sussex Industries Exhibition in Brighton.
- **Marlene Dietrich** winds up more than 2yrs performing for Allied troops with a show at the Olympia Theatre in Paris.

TRAGIC DEATH OF DAVID NIVEN'S WIFE

MAY 21

Primula (Primmie), the wife of actor David Niven, dies after stepping through a doorway at a Hollywood party thinking it is a cloakroom, and falling 20ft into the cellar. The Nivens' romance began in 1940 when he was a British Army officer and she was a WAAF sheltering during an air raid in London. Niven landed on top of her in a trench, and her Pekinese bit him. They married a few weeks later. She also leaves two small sons, David aged 3yrs and Jamie, 6 months.
The family are pictured at Jamie's christening in December 1945.

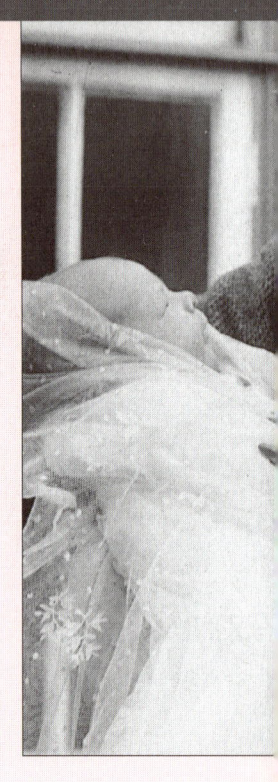

23 Thursday

The **King** attends a one-day match at the Oval to celebrate the centenary of the Surrey County Cricket Club.
- Shouts of 'Bravo', not heard in New York for years, greet the Old Vic's production of *Oedipus*.
- Audiences in Shanghai at *One Night's Kiss* will see the first screen kiss in the history of the Chinese cinema. But out of respect for the public's sense of propriety, the couple in Yasuki Chiba's film do so behind an open parasol.

24 Friday

Sailors from ships of the Home Fleet parade before the **Duke and Duchess of**

MAY

■ After long years of austerity the tools of **glamour** are back for women. Lipsticks, face creams, lotions and nail varnishes will all be available within the next few months.
■ A loincloth, a 'Mae West', a fire extinguisher and two prams are among the **lost property** to be sold if not claimed from Plymouth Lost Property Office.
■ Film star Bing Crosby's brother Larry, claims to have invented a pocket-sized inhaler guaranteed to kill onion, garlic or liquor breath in a few minutes.
. . . ERNEST RHYS (86), writer and editor of the Everyman Library series, dies in London . . .

26 Sunday

Queen Mary (right) celebrates her 79th birthday, and attends the first church parade of the Commando branch of the British Legion at Westminster Abbey.
■ Bread and cakes are unavailable in New York hotels on Tuesday, Wednesday and Thursday evenings until Europe's **food** position improves.
■ The Communists win the general election in Czechoslovakia . . .

27 Monday

Sir Ben Smith resigns as Minister of Food. His successor is Mr John Strachey.
■ During a press conference in Moscow, following the **Big Four** (USA, UK, USSR, France) meeting of foreign ministers in Paris, **Mr Molotov** accuses Britain and the USA of 'using threats, pressure and intimidation' to impose their will on the Soviet Union.
■ Rubber hot water bottle production for the home market is now well in excess of pre-war figures.
. . . Canada's Dionne QUINTUPLETS are 12 today . . .

28 Tuesday

Lord Tedder, Marshal of the Royal Air Force and deputy supreme commander of the

25 Saturday

Windsor in Nice, France, where a statue of Queen Victoria, mutilated by the Germans during the occupation, is unveiled after restoration.
■ Because of the US rail strike, hundreds of **war brides** are stranded aboard their ships in New York until alternative transport can be provided.
■ The Parisian idea to pep up last year's felt beret is to add a ruffle of frothy net which starts at the ear line and goes around the back of the head. Ruffles can be changed to tone with different outfits.

Transjordan becomes an **independent** kingdom called Jordan under the Emir Abdullah.

45

MAY

Allied invasion of Europe, receives the Freedom of the City of London.
■ The General Assembly of the Church of Scotland has set up a committee to consider the possibility of a new translation of the **Bible**. They think the Authorized Version is 'antiquated' and not understood by most people.
. . . Miss D R Allen is appointed RAT CATCHER to Wandsworth Borough Council at a salary of £4.9s.6d. per week, plus a bonus of £1.2s.6d . . .

29 Wednesday

Rail fares go up. The London-Edinburgh return fare is now £6.18s.9d.
■ The Ministry of Supply reveals the **de Havilland Swallow**, the world's first jet-propelled flying-wing fighter plane (the plane is shaped like a wing).
■ A government White Paper projects a shortfall of 26,000 **scientists** in the year 1955, and a country unable to restore its standard of living unless at least one new university is built and there is cash to help double the output of scientists in Britain.
■ Haj Amin al Husseini, the former Grand Mufti of Jerusalem and outstanding leader of the Arabs in Palestine, who fled **Palestine** 8yrs earlier to escape arrest, and after living in Germany under Nazi protection moved to live in France under surveillance, escapes to Egypt by plane.

30 Thursday
New Moon

Food minister John Strachey announces that **bread** will be **rationed** for the first time. Workers in heavy industry will receive a bigger ration than clerical workers (see page 37).
■ **Penguins** return to London Zoo – about 20 of them. Keeper Herbert Jones travelled 3,000 miles from Penguin Islands, just off the Cape, South Africa, to bring them to London.
■ **James Mason**, who used a riding crop on **Margaret Lockwood** in The Man in Grey, hit Dulcie Gray in They Were Sisters and damaged Ann Todd's fingers in The Seventh Veil, is having a rough time himself while making his new film Odd Man Out. He is regularly drenched with water before he goes on set to play a man on the run in all weathers.

31 Friday
Union Day, South Africa

President Truman reveals that Stalin has twice pleaded 'health grounds' when refusing invitations to Washington.
■ **Field Marshal Lord Montgomery** has presented Rommel's pure white Arab charger to the King. Rommel had intended to ride the horse in triumph through Cairo when he had driven the British Army out of Egypt.
■ A '**kitchen robot**', an electric machine that can peel potatoes, clean vegetables and stone fruit, has gone into production in Brno, Czechoslovakia.
. . . BUCKINGHAM PALACE will be lit with coloured floodlights during the victory celebrations . . .

JUNE

1 Saturday

Milkmen in London go on **strike**, asking for minimum weekly wage of £5.4s.6d.

TV'S ON THE WAY

The first post-war **television sets** should be in the shops in the early autumn. Coming from Pye are table models costing £42.17s.3d. and consoles costing £55.2s.6d. The black-and white-pictures will measure about 8in x 6in.

JUNE

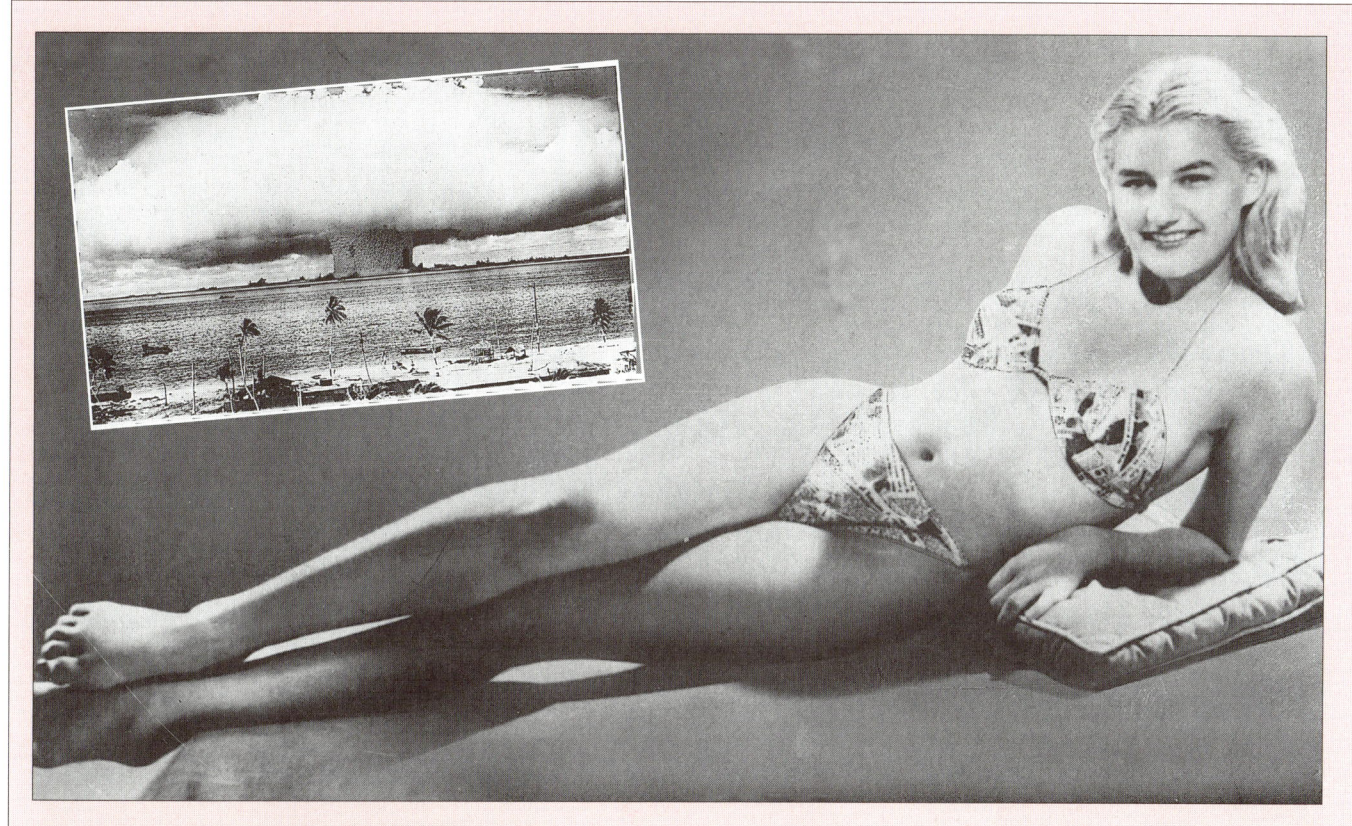

THIS NEW BATHING SUIT IS DYNAMITE!

The 'Bikini' is unveiled in Paris. It has been designed by Louis Reard, a former motor engineer, who named it after the Bikini Atoll, site of the atom bomb test *(inset)*, because he thought his two-piece bathing costume 'highly explosive'. Model Michelene Bernardini gets tons of fan mail and answers each letter with a copy of this picture . . .

■ Hundreds of **sheep** have been driven away and grassland destroyed by a plague of caterpillars covering a square mile of the mountains overlooking Abertilley, Monmouthshire.

■ An **earthquake** wrecks villages in East Turkey. 270 are dead and it is feared there will be many more casualties.

■ The Romanian dictator **Ion Antonescu** is executed in Romania for bringing his country into the Second World War on the side of Germany.

2 Sunday

The Lincoln copy of **Magna Carta** is now permanently installed in a modern safe weighing a ton, and fitted to a concrete block in Lincoln Cathedral.

■ BOAC plan to re-open their North Atlantic service to America on July 1. Fares between London and New York are £92 single, £168 return.

. . . A reward of 3 new-laid eggs or 1s. is offered by a Bognor Regis resident for the return of a clip-on earring . . .

3 Monday

Italy calls a **referendum** on the abolition of the monarchy.

■ The US Supreme Court in Washington, USA, in a decision arising from the case of Irene Morgan, a Negro, who refused to change seats while travelling from Virginia to Baltimore, rules that racial segregation of passengers on inter-state buses is unconstitutional

47

JUNE

LONDON CELEBRATES V-DAY

JUNE 8 V-Day Hundreds of thousands celebrate victory in World War II, lining the route of the gigantic Victory Parade in London, and enthusiastically greeting the Royal Family, who lead the parade with Winston Churchill (Prime Minister during the war, now Leader of the Opposition), the present premier Clement Attlee, and the great war leaders. They are followed by marching columns of Empire and Allied servicemen and civilians, accompanied by the massed bands of the Army, Navy and Air Force. In the Mall, the King takes the Victory Parade salute and, later, cheering crowds call their majesties again and again onto the balcony of Buckingham Palace. Even heavy rain towards the end of the afternoon does not dampen the people's enjoyment of fireworks and floodlight displays, and bonfires blaze from the West End to Wapping – there is singing and dancing in the streets all night.

JUNE

49

JUNE

4 Tuesday

Detective story writers are invited to have a look at the Police Exhibition in Brighton by the Home Secretary, **Mr Chuter Ede**, when he opens it today. 'They are apt to fall into major errors when they come to describe how the police actually do their work.'

■ **Princess Elizabeth** and **Princess Margaret** go to Eton College, Windsor, Berks, where they are chief guests at the College's Fourth of June celebrations.

■ 'Amenities first,' says West Suffolk County Council, which is allowing telephone wires to be put up where famous English artist **John Constable** painted.

5 Wednesday

The Derby, back at Epsom for the first time in six years, is won by *Airborne (right)*, a 50-1 outsider, ridden by T Lowrey and owned by Mr Ferguson.

■ A majority of nearly 2 million Italians vote to end the 85yr-reign of the House of Savoy. and become a republic. **Umberto II** has been king for only 29 days *(see May 9)*.

■ One-way traffic is to be abolished in Bath, Somerset because 'it applies sedan-chair conditions to a jet-propelled age'.

6 Thursday

MPs in the House of Commons hear letters from the former Italian Ambassador, Count Dino Guardi, written in 1934 and 1935, disclosing that **Mussolini** subsidised Oswald Mosley's British Union of Fascists at the rate of £60,403 a year.

■ The official figures of Britain's World War II **casualties** are: Armed forces 357,116 killed, 6,244 missing, 369.267 wounded and 184,072 imprisoned or interned; Civilians - 60,595 killed.

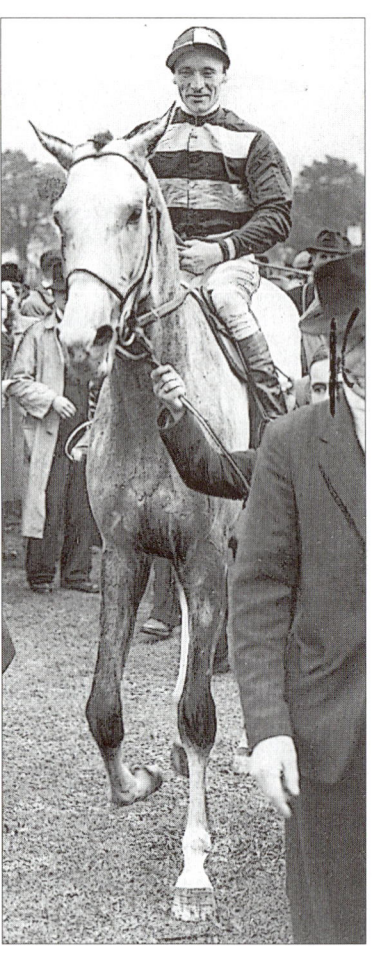

7 Friday

Dai Rees wins the Spalding £1,500 Professional Golf Tournament at St Andrews, finishing one stroke ahead of Henry Cotton and R A Whitcombe. There are 260 entries for the Open Championship, which begins in the first week of July.

■ America bans *The Wicked Lady* in its present form because the film's name part, played by **Margaret Lockwood**, cheats on her marriage. The film was one of 1945's roaring successes in Britain.

■ 'Holiday strollers, watch your step,' warns the War Office. About 800,000 tons of ammunitions and **explosives** still lie beside country roads and in fields and forests. It will take at least 3yrs to clear it all.

8 Saturday

V-Day. Hundreds of thousands celebrate victory in World War II, lining the route of the gigantic Victory Parade in London *(see pages 48-49)*.

■ England's Rugby League touring team beats New South Wales 21-7 in Sydney, Australia.

9 Sunday
Whitsun

King Ananda Mahidol of Siam (20) is found shot dead in his palace in Bangkok, Siam *(see panel, facing page)*.

■ 'Best behaved ever' is the Ministry of Works verdict on London's **V-Day crowds**, which topped 12 million. 2,500,000 teas and lemonades were sold with 2,000,000 sandwiches and 1,200,000 buns.

10 Monday

Moscow Radio makes its first reference to the **Victory** celebrations in London with a brief description of the parade.

■ Following the **referendum** results, Italy

50

JUNE

"BOY" KING OF SIAM FOUND SHOT DEAD

JUNE 9

King Ananda Mahidol of Siam (20) is found shot dead in his palace in Bangkok, Siam. The shy, music-loving king also held the titles of Brother of the Moon, Supreme Arbiter of the Ebb and Flow of the Tide and Possessor of the Four and Twenty Golden Umbrellas. He succeeded to the throne at the age of seven, and spent the war years in Lausanne, Switzerland. He returned to Siam only six months ago after an absence of 13yrs.

is to become a republic, but King Umberto II refuses to go, alleging poll irregularities. (See May 9 and June 5)
■ The **Labour Party Conference** opens in Bournemouth.
. . . Nearly 120,000 schoolchildren in London, Surrey, Kent and Herts will have a day's outing this week to a theatre, circus or rodeo, arranged for them by the LCC . . .

11 Tuesday

'V' stamps go with a rush – 24 million 3d. and 240 million 2½d. stamps have been sold.
■ Ten thousand Italian **Monarchists** lay siege to Communist HQ in Naples, Italy, after failing to storm the building with Molotov cocktails. Police and troops join battle with them, and at least 8 people are killed and 50 injured.
■ Using jet engines in the hull of his old Bluebird II, **Sir Malcolm Campbell** (60), plans to make another bid for the world's motor-boat speed record this autumn.
■ Mrs Mattie Lyons Large (79) who has 49 grandchildren, has married Delbert Sprouse (18), in Louisa, Kentucky.

12 Wednesday

The King's Birthday Honours List: **Admiral Lord Louis Mountbatten** is made a Viscount, and the **Earl of Halifax** receives the Order of Merit.
■ Extra police are called in to control thousands of **sightseers** waiting outside Westminster Abbey for the **wedding** (below) of the Duke of Northumberland to Lady Elizabeth Montague Douglas Scott, daughter of the Duke of Buccleuch. The Royal Family are among the guests.
■ The Italian government issues a statement supporting the establishment of a republic, and Premier Alcide de Gasperi assumes the duties of Head of State.
■ New York's 7,500,000 people set up a record with 14,108,853 phone calls in one day.

13 Thursday

Ex-**King Umberto II** of Italy leaves for exile in Portugal. In a message to the Italian people, he accuses the new government of a 'revolutionary act' confronting him with the alternative of provoking bloodshed or submitting to violence. (See May 9, June 5 & 10)

JUNE

■ The trial of 28 Japanese war leaders begins in Tokyo.
■ **Mannequins** are piped in at a Regent Street, London, store showing the colourful non-austerity wool dresses inspired by the Highlands, which are to be one of this Autumn's fashion highlights.
. . . A miniature tornado sweeps across Suffolk, causing floods and leaving Bury St Edmunds without electricity for 5 hours . . .

14 Friday
Full Moon

Houses designed to save walking, with a combined kitchen, living room and scullery, and a 3-in-1 cooker, heater and boiler are being ordered in their thousands by councils in Shropshire and Montgomeryshire. They cost £1,474 each.
■ The death is announced of TV pioneer, **John Logie Baird** (58). He was the first person to show television pictures of objects in motion and his system was used for experimental transmissions in both Britain and Germany. But when the BBC started its new television service in 1936 it elected to use the Marconi-EMI system in preference to Baird's. He also invented 'Noctovisor' for seeing in the dark by invisible rays.

15 Saturday

British actor/director **Laurence Olivier** *(facing page)* is awarded an honorary degree of Master of Arts at Tufts University, Boston, USA, for his outstanding contribution to the art of the cinema.
■ Objections from the Roosevelt family have cost American actor Lionel Barrymore the role of Franklin D Roosevelt in the forthcoming atom bomb film *The Beginning of the End*. The family is opposed to him because he didn't support Roosevelt in the 1944 presidential campaign.
■ **Suspender belts** with poems on them and panties for jitterbug dancers emblazoned with comments like 'Touch Down' and 'Remember Me' are among the exhibits at the Corset and Brassiere Guild Show in America.

16 Sunday

Prime Minister Attlee reveals plans for united Indian independence, and invites India to set up an interim government of 14 members. **Pandit Nehru** *(above)* would be deputy to the Viceroy and hold the portfolio of External Afairs.
■ The first **holiday** for 6yrs is being enjoyed by 500 children at the LCC's Martello Holiday Camp at Walton, Essex.
■ During the first year of demobilisation, over 3 million new outfits were issued, and during January this year 100,000 men and 5 tons of clothing were passing through the depots weekly.

17 Monday

Following their destruction of eight road and rail bridges linking Palestine and Jordan, Jewish **terrorists** blow up Palestine railways' central workshops in the Haifa Bay area and a road bridge near the Syrian border.
■ The US Treasury List reveals that **Carmen Miranda**, the snake-hipped screen dancer known for her exotic headdresses, earned £50,364 last year. Highest paid man, with £278,258, is Leo McCarey, director of *The Bells of St Mary's* and *Going My Way*. Other stars listed

JUNE

include Ray Milland with £60,833, Paulette Goddard with £46,833 and Betty Grable with £43,000.
- The Allies decide not to try **Emperor Hirohito** of Japan as a war criminal.

18 Tuesday

Royal Ascot starts today. The King has ordered that uniforms and lounge suits are the correct wear for men in the Royal Enclosure.
- There is a **curfew** in Palestine after Jewish terrorists kidnap 5 British officers and 3 others who were guests at a club established by the Jews to extend hospitality to Allied troops in Tel Aviv.

19 Wednesday

Prime Minister Attlee tells the House of Commons that Sunday November 10 will be observed as Armistice Day for both World War I and II..
- US **President Truman** urges Congress to authorise immediately an addition $465million to UNRRA as millions overseas are still threatened with disaster.
- *Friar's Fancy* ridden by E Smith and owned by Mr O V Watney wins the Royal Hunt Cup at Ascot in heavy rain.
- In New York's Yankee Stadium, **Joe Louis** (USA) knocks out Billy Conn (USA) in the eighth round to retain the world heavyweight crown *(pictures, page 42)*.

20 Thursday

The US State of Georgia begins court proceedings against the **Ku Klux Klan**, charging it with conspiracy to seize key government agencies and employing propaganda for 'violence, terrorism and hate' against the negro population. The Klan reached its zenith in the 1920s when it had 4 million supporters, but after declining throughout the 30s began to revive with the outbreak of World War II, when it became noted for its Fascist sympathies. It was disbanded in 1944, but continues on a local level.
- The 'best horse in France', *Caracalla*, ridden by C Elliott and owned by M Boussac wins the Gold Cup at Ascot.

21 Friday

Special buses take 8,000 children to Birmingham Town Hall to hear the city orchestra, which gives them a lesson in classical music.
- Australia will supply Britain with 30 million dozen **eggs** and 10,000 tons of egg pulp this year. Before the war the average shipment was 12 million dozen eggs a year.
- Eighteen British films are to be shown as 'prestige pictures' in an American distribution plan following the huge success of *Henry V* starring Laurence Olivier.

22 Saturday

Senator Theodor Bilbo of Mississippi (USA) has called on all 'red-blooded Anglo-Saxon men' to stop **negroes voting** in the July 2 elections. Religious bodies start a petition asking President Truman to send troops to Mississippi to protect the negroes.
- Six hundred servicemen, WRNS and ATS stage a **sit-down protest** in Piccadilly, London against the proposed closure of the Stage Door Canteen service, causing a massive West End hold-up.

OLIVIERS ESCAPE IN AIR DRAMA

**DATELINE: June 18
The engine drops off and a wing catches fire on a Pan American plane carrying British actors Laurence Olivier and his wife, Vivien Leigh, to London at the end of the Old Vic Company's triumphant season in America, where Olivier has also been feted for his film** *Henry V*. **The pilot crash lands on a small airfield in Connecticut and none of the 42 passengers and 10 crew is hurt.**

JUNE

A Glory Year For England

The MCC cricketers pictured in Southampton before departing for their winter tour to Australia. The tour follows a hugely successful home series against India, which they win convincingly. And they sign off 1946 in fine style Down Under, winning the first Test by a remarkably comfortable margin of an innings and 215 runs.

23 Sunday

The Board of Trade announces that nearly 50 internal airline routes will link British cities. The new services will be run by the projected British European Airways Corporation.

■ Ten Commandos, selected at random from the audience, sit with the Queen, Princess Elizabeth, Princess Margaret and the Duchess of Kent in the Royal Box at the Albert Hall concert in aid of the Commandos' Benevolent Fund.

. . . Sunburn Sunday for Britain except the Midlands and Yorkshire which, true to form, have storms and rain . . .

24 Monday

In New York, the UN Security Council votes 7-4 against breaking off diplomatic relations with Franco's Spain, but defers the decision to the September meeting of the General Assembly.

■ **Morris Cars** raise the price of their 2-door saloon car to £270. The 4-door model will cost £290.

■ Brighter upholstery, with red leather arm rests, is being fitted in London's **Underground** carriages.

■ **William S Hart** (73), silent screen cowboy star of such classic films as *Wolves of the Trail*, *Blue Blazes*, *Rawden*, *Tumbleweed* and many others, dies in Los Angeles, USA.

25 Tuesday

CRICKET: England win the first Test match against India by 10 wickets at Lords.

■ According to a White Paper, 695,000 people were employed in all Government

54

JUNE

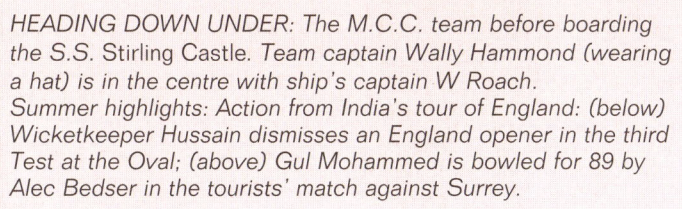

HEADING DOWN UNDER: The M.C.C. team before boarding the S.S. Stirling Castle. Team captain Wally Hammond (wearing a hat) is in the centre with ship's captain W Roach. Summer highlights: Action from India's tour of England: (below) Wicketkeeper Hussain dismisses an England opener in the third Test at the Oval; (above) Gul Mohammed is bowled for 89 by Alec Bedser in the tourists' match against Surrey.

departments on April 1 this year. Moscow Radio says that Russia has exported 4 million bottles of **champagne** this year.

■ A man at Pembroke assizes, who said that his marriage had been wrecked by the 'dominating personality' of his mother-in-law, aided by his father-in-law, is awarded £150 damages against them for the enticement of his wife.

26 Wednesday

Princess Elizabeth and **Princess Margaret** visit the film set of *Nicholas Nickleby* at Ealing Studios in London and meet 6ft 6in Australian actor **Chips Rafferty**, *right*, and famous American gossip columnist, Hedda Hopper. They also watch several takes of a scene from a new film *Hue and Cry*.

■ The Duke and Duchess of Gloucester attend the Hollywood-style premiere in Sydney of the first film to be produced in Australia by Columbia Pictures. *Smithy* tells the story of the late Sir Charles Kingsford-Smith, the famous Australian airman.

■ Crooner **Rudy Vallee** sings *The Long, Long Trail* and *The Last Round-Up* at the funeral of silent screen Western star, William S Hart, in San Francisco today.

27 Thursday

Holiday-makers are recommended to bring their own **towels**, sheets and soap, according to the Margate Hotel Keepers' Association letter to visitors.

JUNE

■ **Sir John Shelley-Rolls**, great nephew of the English poet Percy Bysshe Shelley, has given his collection of Shelly manuscripts to the Bodleian Library, Oxford, together with five notebooks and more than 100 letters belonging to his wife, Mary Shelley, who is most famous as the author of *Frankenstein*.

■ Thirty Jewish **terrorists** are sentenced to 15yr jail terms in Jerusalem. The prisoners in the dock sing resistance songs, while hysterical relatives wail in the public galleries.

28 Friday

The last of the **wheelchairs** which used to ply for hire in Bath, Somerset, and to which the city gave its name, is sent to a museum by its licensed owner. As recently as 1908, there were 66 licensed chairs in Bath, but the rise of motor traffic had reduced the number to 3 by 1940.

■ Two hundred greengrocers queue outside the gates of Brentford Market in Middlesex in the hope of buying cherries, but by 7am they had all gone.

29 Saturday
New Moon

Winston Churchill is to give all members of the wartime coalition government a commemorative bronze medallion. On one side is inscribed 'Salute the Great Coalition, 1940-1945, and on the other side appears the name of the recipient and 'from Winston Churchill'.

■ **President Sukarno** of Indonesia declares martial law in Java, and calls on his countrymen to free Indonesia (the Dutch East Indies) from the Dutch.

■ The great Italian conductor, **Arturo Toscanini** (left) won't go to Paris to conduct the Milan orchestra, and his London concerts planned for later this year are in doubt, because he is annoyed with the Big Four (UK, USA, USSR and France) over their decision to give North Italy's Briga and Tenda regions to France.

30 Sunday

It is National Baby Week in Britain. It is estimated that more than 17,000 babies will be born this week in England and Wales alone.

■ A **'Sweetheart' Bill**, allowing foreigners engaged to US servicemen or women to enter America to marry, has been signed by President Truman.

■ America conducts its fourth **Atomic bomb** test at Bikini Atoll, in the Pacific. Three ships placed in the target area are sunk and 31 out of the other 73 anchored there are damaged.

JULY

CROWDS FLOCK BACK TO THE CENTRE COURT

The first person in the all-night queue at **WIMBLEDON** (the first since 1939) gets a Centre Court view of the Frenchman Yvon Petra *(above)* beating Geoff Brown (Australia) to win the men's singles crown 6-2, 6-4, 7-9, 5-7, 6-4. Next day, Pauline Betz, USA *(facing page)* **beats compatriot Louise Brough 6-2, 6-4 to claim the ladies' title.**

JULY

1 Monday
Dominion Day, Canada

More than 5,000 Jews, including all the leaders of the Jewish Agency, have been arrested in the 36hrs since the British started their **anti-terrorist campaign** in Palestine. Prime Minister Attlee defends the action, saying Britain can no longer tolerate the loss of life and material damage - 21 lives and £4 million since last December.

■ **IBM** in New York demonstrates an electrically operated Chinese language typewriter that can type 5,400 characters horizontally or vertically.

■ **Lord Woolton** accepts Winston Churchill's invitation to become Chairman of the Conservative Party. He made his name during the war at the Ministry of Food, where he was charged with seeing the nation was well nourished.

2 Tuesday

British troops in **Palestine** discover a massive cache of arms at Mesheq Yagour belonging to the Haganah, the Jewish underground army, which has been responsible for much destruction of property and armed resistance.

■ Four out of five households have taken out a **radio licence**, which will bring in £10 million a year. The government pledges more money for the development of BBC home radio and television programmes.

. . . The hottest day of the year. It's 87°F in London . . .

3 Wednesday

The **Jockey Club**, the select body that controls horse racing in England, announces that photo finish cameras will be installed on all racecourses.

■ **Herrings** are swarming round the Shetland Islands, Scotland. Boats landed four million yesterday and today.

■ There are 3,700,000 **bachelors** in the USA, 300,000 below normal because of the war, says the Chief of the US Census Bureau (who happens to be a woman).

. . . The last British troops will leave Denmark on August 31 . . .

4 Thursday
Independence Day, USA

Champagne will soon be on sale in Britain at £1.10s. per bottle, following an agreement with France, who has guaranteed to send 150,000 cases this year.

■ America gives the **Philippine Islands**

57

JULY

their independence after 48yrs of American administration. Manuel Roxas becomes their first president.
■ British Metropolitan Vickers win the contract to build a £4,230,000 electricity **power station** in Turkey.
■ The **Big Four** foreign ministers (UK, USA, USSR and France) meeting in Paris agree to call a Peace Conference on July 29.

5 Friday

45,000 women engineers, meeting at Manchester's Trafford Park Industrial Estate, loudly cheer suggestions for a 'new suffragette movement' to win **equal pay** for equal work.
■ Canada is shipping more than 4.5 million tons of **grain** to Britain, the Empire and Europe to ease the grain shortage.
■ American golfer 'Slammin'' **Sam Snead** (below) wins The Open Championship at St Andrews, Scotland.

6 Saturday

Anyone reading Kathleen Winsor's *Forever Amber* in the state of Massachusetts, USA, is liable to 2yrs imprisonment, a fine of £350, or both, because the state has banned the novel as being '**obscene**, indecent and impure'.
■ The **jam** prospects are good this year – fruit crops are as good as usual, says the Ministry of Food.

7 Sunday

After Pope Pius XII canonises Mother Frances Cabrini, the first American citizen to be made a **saint**, a plane drops photographs of her and bunches of violets, the new saint's favourite flower, to the thousands waiting in St Peter's Square, Rome. Known as the 'Sister of the Immigrants', Mother Cabrini worked in the USA from 1889 until her death in Chicago in 1917.
■ For the first time since 1939, **luxury goods** such as cosmetics, toys, sports gear, artificial silks and jelly powder are to be imported from America.
. . . Madame Leanne Lanvin, (79), leading Paris dress designer, dies . . .

8 Monday

Margaret Hilda Roberts (above, right, with her family) of Grantham, an undergraduate at Somerville College, Oxford, is elected president of the Oxford University Conservatives.
■ The British government is making a gift of £20 million to the island of **Malta** to help in its reconstruction after the devastation it suffered in World War II.
■ A man in East London, South Africa shot a hare and threw it into the back of his car. The hare woke up, touched off the gun as it leaped for the window and shot the motorist in the neck. The man recovered. The hare escaped.

9 Tuesday

The Countess Ciano, **Mussolini's daughter**, is released from compulsory domicile in the Lipari

Islands as part of the **amnesty** declared to celebrate the inauguration of the Italian republic.
■ The King and Queen give a **garden party** at Buckingham Palace for 7,000 guests.
. . . Lord Louis Mountbatten is given the Freedom of the City of London . . .

10 Wednesday

The British Foreign Secretary at a meeting in Paris says the Four powers must cooperate to govern Germany.
■ The Board of Trade says more **reptile skins** will be imported to make shoes.
■ The **Ticket Punching** Championship takes place this weekend at the London Transport Gala in Walthamstow, London.
. . . JACKIE PATERSON (GB) retains the World, Empire and British fly-weight titles, when he wins every round to outpoint Joe Curran (GB) at Hampden Park, Glasgow . . .

11 Thursday

Cagney Productions, set up by US film star **James Cagney** (above), famous for playing many tough guy and gangster roles including *Public Enemy, Angels with Dirty Faces, Love Me or Leave Me*, and for his dancing in *Yankee Doodle Dandy* (for which he won an Oscar), has signed up **Audie Murphy** (22), holder of the Congressional Medal of Honour and World War II's most decorated GI.
■ Jim Moran of California, hatches a 1lb 9oz **ostrich** by sitting on the egg for 23 days. Moran says 'It took a lot of warmth and determination, but it is worth it. He looks just like me.'
■ **Henry Cotton** wins the French Open golf tournament in Paris.
. . . Heat wave: London is the hottest spot with 83°F.

12 Friday

The **Big Four** Foreign Ministers (UK, USA, USSR, France) end their Paris talks with the major issues of Germany and Austria undecided, and minor issues left for the July Peace Conference (*see July 4*) to solve.
■ The **Hairdressers'** Guild warns ex-servicemen and women against investing their hard-earned £50 and £100 gratuities in 5 or 6 month hairdressing or beauty courses, saying it takes at least 3yrs to learn the job properly.
■ A new opera, *The Rape of Lucretia*, by English composer **Benjamin Britten** (*below*), who established himself as an opera composer of the first importance with *Peter Grimes* in 1945, re-opens the Glyndebourne Festival Opera House. Kathleen Ferrier, Owen Brannigan and Peter Pears are among the cast.
. . . HEAT WAVE: London swelters in 88°F . . .

13 Saturday

The US House of Representatives ratifies the **loan** of £937 million to Britain by 219 votes to 155, after a week's strenuous debate (*see May 10*).
■ The Ministry of Works estimates that 2 million new houses will be built by the end of the year – a rather better record than the 170 built in the year following the end of the 1914-18 war.
■ The **King and Queen** give their second garden party of the week, this time for 2,500 of their tenants at Sandringham.
■ Film stars **Anne Baxter** and **John**

JULY

Hodiak marry in California. She is the grand-daughter of the great American architect Frank Lloyd Wright, and her films include *The Magnificent Ambersons* and the forthcoming *The Razor's Edge*. He has starred in *Ziegfeld Follies* and *A Bell for Adano*.

14 Sunday
Full Moon

The King unveils a **Cross of Sacrifice** in the services plot laid out by the Imperial War Graves Commission in Great Bircham churchyard on the Sandringham estate.
■ Thousands of people visit Bognor Regis, Sussex, every day in the hope of seeing the Meteor jet planes that are preparing to attack the world speed record. But many residents are complaining about the low-flying 600mph roar.

15 Monday
St Swithin's Day

The **National Coal Board**, the body through which the state will run the industry, comes into being. Its first action is to send a poster to every mine and to all members of the National Union of Miners with the slogan 'ALL PULL TOGETHER'.
■ **General Draja Mihailovich**, the former Yugoslav guerrilla leader, is sentenced to death in Belgrade, Yugoslavia, for treason and collaboration. The general initially led the Chetniks against the occupying German and Italian troops. He joined forces with Tito, but when Tito won the support of the Allies, he switched his allegiance to the Germans and Italians in a bid to defeat the Communists.

16 Tuesday

The **petrol ration** is increased by 50%. This means that each driver will be able to drive 270 miles per month, instead of the present 180 miles.
■ The death sentence is passed on 43 German SS men at **Dachau**, Germany, for the murder of 900 US soldiers and Belgian civilians.
■ Twentieth Century Fox, the American film company, has signed up the 20yr-old photographic model **Norma Jean Baker** *(left)* at a salary of $75 a week. She will be known professionally as Marilyn Monroe.
■ 200 million Belgian bricks have arrived in Britain to form the basis of a brick pool to meet any shortage in the house-building programme.

17 Wednesday

Five **bombs** explode in the British Services Club in Alexandria, Egypt, injuring 25 people. The Egyptian Prime Minister, Sidky Pasha, offers a reward of £5,000 for information leading to arrest of those responsible for this 'dastardly act'.
■ **General Mihailovich** *(see July 15)* is executed by firing squad in Belgrade, Yugoslavia.

18 Thursday

Thousands of New Yorkers have their first sight of Britain's famous RAF '35' bomber squadron as 12 **Lancasters**, which arrived in America yesterday on a goodwill visit, fly in V-formation over the city and Long Island.
■ **Michael Rennie** (35) the 6ft 2in Yorkshire-born film actor, signs a five-film contract worth £300,000 – the most lucrative contract ever offered to a British actor in British films.
■ The RAF's newest jet fighter, the de Havilland Vampire, will be unveiled at the Paris Air Show that opens on July 21.

JULY

TERRORIST BOMBS HIT JERUSALEM

DATELINE: JULY 22
A WING of the King David Hotel in Jerusalem, HQ of the British Army in Palestine, is destroyed by a terrorist time bomb. 48 are reported dead, 76 missing and 58 injured. The explosives were packed in milk churns which were delivered to the Regency Restaurant under the offices of the Army. The head of the Palestine CID says, 'it has all the earmarks of the Stern Gang'.

19 Friday

Clothes manufacturers are putting fun into utility fabrics with gay woolly lambs skipping across coloured backgrounds, rows of sailors on parade, or baskets of coloured fruit.

■ Film star **Greta Garbo** is home in Sweden on a 'purely private visit', after 8yrs in America. The legendary Swedish film star (*Queen Christina, Camille, Anna Karenina*, etc) has made just two films since 1938: *Ninotchka*, celebrated for the publicity slogan 'Garbo laughs', and *Two-Faced Woman*, which was denounced by the US Legion of Decency as 'immoral and un-Christian'. Changes made it a critical failure.

20 Saturday

Britain is drawing £75 million of the US loan immediately *(see July 13)*. The first priority is mining machinery; the second is food, including oranges, lemons, dried eggs, tinned salmon and pilchards.

61

JULY

■ Women teachers protest at Middlesex County Council's advertisements for 'headmasters'. The Council agrees that in future women as well as men can be heads of mixed schools.

21 Sunday

Opponents of Sunday cricket at Amersham, Bucks, tell the parish council that allowing cricket to be played will mean opening the door to Sunday cinema as well.

■ The Home Secretary, Mr Chuter Ede, is to examine a proposal by the British Spiritualists' Union to abolish the **Witchcraft** Act of 1735, under which a person can be charged with 'pretending to be a medium'.

■ The International Grand Prix race in Geneva, Switzerland, is won by Farena of Italy driving an Alfa Romeo. The only British car to finish the race is an ERA driven by Prince Birabongse.

AMERICA'S A-BOMB TESTS ROCK BIKINI ATOLL

An artist's impression of the three stages in the progress of the bomb burst at Bikini Atoll on July 24. The mushroom cloud reaches 60,000 feet within six minutes of the explosion on the Pacific island. Within 20 minutes there is a period of severe atmospheric disturbance and dangerous radioactivity as the cloud reaches its maximum height.

22 Monday

Bread and flour **rationing** starts today.

■ **Emmanuel Shinwell**, Minister of Fuel & Power, warns that there is **not enough coal** to get Britain through the winter.

23 Tuesday

■ Twentieth Century Fox studios announce that **Linda Darnell** (right), the dark-eyed, sultry actress whose films include *The Mark of Zorro* and *Blood and Sand*, is to replace Peggy Cummins in the starring role in *Forever Amber*. Miss Cummins was sacked as she looked too young for the part (see May 19).

■ Two million New Yorkers stage a buyers' strike against **soaring prices**. Demonstrations take every possible form, from planes spelling out slogans in the sky, to film actors collecting signatures.

24 Wednesday

America conducts the first underwater **atom bomb test** at Bikini Atoll in the South Pacific (see panel, above).

■ **Dr Edith Summerskill**, Parliamentary Under-Secretary at the Ministry of Food, gives the first real definition of haggis, while explaining the reason it is off the ration list.

JULY

■ Gift parcels for Britain, usually containing food, are being handed in at post offices in New Zealand at the rate of 12,000 a week.

25 Thursday

The Irish Parliament, the Dail, agrees that **Eire** should apply to join the United Nations. Premier Eamon de Valera, says that Britain supports the application.
■ Princess Elizabeth and **Princess Margaret** (below) take their first ride on a public transport bus when, with 25 other Sea-rangers, they are driven from Dartmouth to Brixham and back.

26 Friday

The Gaelic League opposes Irish Premier de Valera's idea that British tourists should be encouraged to come to Eire, because they fear that the hotels that would be built would become strongholds 'to spread and foster English.'
■ Irish playwright **George Bernard Shaw**, among whose classic plays are *Pygmalion, The Apple Cart, St Joan, Caesar* and *Cleopatra, Man & Superman* and *Major Barbara*, celebrates his 90th birthday.
■ Heavy **rain** sweeps the country, and causes crop damage from the Isle of Wight to Yorkshire.

27 Saturday

The Governor of Georgia, USA, is offering a reward of $10,000 for information leading to conviction of the participants in a **lynching** nr Monroe, Georgia, on Thursday of two negro farmhands and their wives. He describes the killings as, 'one of the worst incidents ever to take place in our state'.
■ **Lord Nuffield**, car maker and philanthropist, gives St Dunstan's £10,000 for research into scientific aids for the blind.

28 Sunday
New Moon

Traffic is held up in London's West End by a £1 million pageant of motoring during the past 50yrs. The parade is 1½ miles long. The King and Queen later inspect the vehicles at the world's largest motor show in Regents Park.
■ **Petula Clark**, 13, (right) is such a hit in Wesley Ruggles' new Technicolor film musical *London Town* that Ruggles gives her a film contract.

29 Monday

The Moslem League in India, withdraws its acceptance of the British Cabinet's long-term plans for a united India, and reverts to its demand for a separate and fully sovereign state of Pakistan. It threatens to take direct action if necessary.
■ A huge bas-relief of the King of Assyria after his victory over the Israelites, 2,600yrs-old and weighing half a ton, is sold at Sotheby's for £3,500.
■ In America, the New York Justice Department revokes the **Ku Klux Klan** charter (see June 20) and reveals that it is investigating Klan activities in New York, Michigan, Tennessee, Florida, California, Mississippi and Georgia.
. . . Opening of the Paris Peace Conference . . .

30 Tuesday

Good news for **divorcees**: from today the decree absolute will be granted 6 weeks after the decree nisi, not six months as previously.
■ **Queen Wilhelmina** of the Netherlands arrives in England with 36 Netherlands horses – 6 greys and 30 blacks – which she will present to the King. Most of them are for use by the Household Cavalry.

AUGUST

31 Wednesday

The British government approves an Anglo-American plan for the partition of Palestine.
■ American **G-men** are combing 7 southern states of the USA for Ku Klux Klan members in a bid to end racial lynchings. Five negroes are reported killed in the past week, and the Klan is being outlawed *(see June 20 and July 29)*.
... The ban on marriages between British soldiers and German women is lifted ...

AUGUST

1 Thursday

British European Airways comes into being.
■ Accident-free Norwich, Norfolk, is asked for tips by London **road safety** officers in Westminster, Hammersmith, Chelsea and Kensington.
■ Film producer Sydney Box takes control of Gainsborough Pictures, Britain's most successful film production company, whose stars include James Mason, Stewart Granger, Patricia Roc, Phyllis Calvert, Dennis Price, Jean Kent and Margaret Lockwood.

2 Friday

Adolf Hitler's £1 million, 3,000 ton luxury yacht *Grille* is for sale in Germany, to anyone who has £75,000 to spare and the £1,000 per week it costs to run it.
■ A **skeleton** unearthed at Figheldean, nr Marlborough, Wilts, is said by experts to be that of a man who died 2,000 years ago.
■ After years of being banned by the Nazis, the **Salvation Army** is attracting large crowds to their street services in Frankfurt, Germany.

3 Saturday

People who 'use and enjoy' Grosvenor Square, London, will be able to claim **compensation** from Westminster Council for the loss of their rights, when a statue of the late President Roosevelt is erected there.
■ The Isle of Ely, Cambs, has decided that no children will be **exempted** from school to work on the land.

4 Sunday

The Queen's **birthday**. She is 46. The King and Queen celebrate her birthday with a picnic in Windsor Forest, with the Duchess of Kent.
■ Cuba protests to the Big Four foreign ministers (UK, USA, USSR, France) at being excluded from the Paris Peace Conference of 21 nations which opened on July 29.
... The government proposes that the salaries of the governors of the BBC are cut to £600 a year ...

5 Monday

Bank Holiday.

Dry **warm** weather brings the biggest bank holiday rush to the sea for 7yrs. The temperature reaches 83°F at Blackpool.
■ The first **Family Allowances** are payable this week to mothers with children under school-leaving age.
■ Supplementary **rations** of bread, fats and meat will be provided for all city inhabitants in the British zone of Germany to bring the daily ration from 1,137 to 1,337 calories a day.
■ The first of the 'people's' cars to reach the German people have been delivered by the British-controlled factory at Fallersleben for the use of a public authority. Since production was converted from war purposes, the 'people's' car has been produced in large numbers for the military.

TOP SONGS OF 1946

PITY TO SAY GOODNIGHT – Dorothy Squires
THE BELLS OF ST MARY'S – Bing Crosby
I WANT TO SEE THE PEOPLE HAPPY – from Big Ben
LA VIE EN ROSE – Edith Piaf
LAUGHING ON THE OUTSIDE CRYING ON THE INSIDE
    – Dorothy Squires
TO EACH HIS OWN – The Inkspots
ZIP A DEE DO DAH – from Song of the South
THE CHARM OF YOU – Frank Sinatra
CHICKARY CHICK – Carol Gibbons Orchestra with
    Rita Wiliams (soloist)
CRUISIN' DOWN THE RIVER – Lou Praeger and his
    Orchestra
DID YOU EVER GET THAT FEELING IN THE
    MOONLIGHT   Perry Como
HER BATHING SUIT NEVER GOT WET – Andrews Sisters
YOU ALWAYS HURT THE ONE YOU LOVE
    – Spike Jones and his City Slickers.

AUGUST

PRINCESS ELIZABETH AT THE EISTEDDFOD

DATELINE: August 6
PRINCESS ELIZABETH is invested as an honorary Ovate of the Gorsedd of Bards of Wales at the Eisteddfod Festival at Cynon Valley, Glamorgan, under the title Elizabeth of Windsor.

6 Tuesday

Britain will receive 96,300,000lbs of butter this year from Denmark, which also hopes to send us a total of 91,300,000lbs of bacon.
■ **Princess Elizabeth** is invested as an honorary Ovate at the Gorsedd of Bards of Wales at the Eisteddfod festival *(see panel)*.

7 Wedneday

There are 82 cases of **typhoid** in Aberystwyth, Wales, and a hotel on the seafront has been commandeered to house volunteers brought in to fight the epidemic.
■ **Gas strike** in London: 10 gasworks and 2,000 men are involved in a dispute over wages.
  . . . Britain tells the US it will not allow any more illegal entries to Palestine . . .

8 Thursday

British wives joining their husbands in Germany are warned not to enter the Russian sector alone. If they go in without their husbands, they are liable to be arrested.

65

AUGUST

THEY KNOW the drill by now: Fred Lewington and his daughter rescue dinner from their basement flat in Kilburn, London. It is the seventh time they have been flooded out. This year, Holmfirth, Yorks, *(above)* suffers £1m of damage in May when the River Holme bursts its banks; in September, it's a struggle to get to work in west London *(right)*; Maidenhead is awash in December when the Thames overflows, leaving a boatman to rescue a stranded driver *(below right)*; in November, the phrase 'holy water' takes on a new meaning *(below, centre)* as Plympton Parish Church, Devon, is isolated in just one hour by flood waters that reach 4ft deep in the churchyard. The vicar looks forlornly at his stock of ruined bibles. Prayers had been offered for the harvest, but in Perth, Scotland *(below)*, it becomes more a question of salvaging what you can from the quagmire and for some, like this collie in Chertsey, Surrey, in December *(below, left)* it's a case of getting in the bath to avoid getting wet . . .

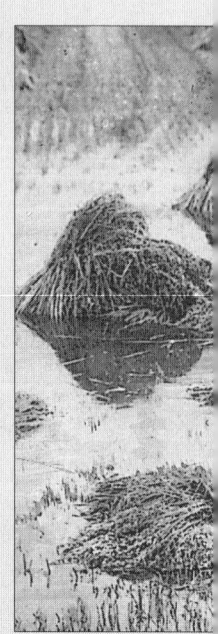

66

AUGUST

1946 – The Year of Flood Misery

67

AUGUST

9 Friday

■ **Persia** protests to the government about British troops being sent to Basra, Iraq, to protect British interests in the Persian Gulf, and demands their immediate withdrawal.

The first ever totally accurate **map** of its kind, just issued by the Admiralty, shows the shortest route from London to any part of the world as a straight line, a great aid to air navigators.

■ Australia hopes to have an **immigration** scheme in shape by the New Year. 90,000 Britons have already applied to go there.

■ A serious situation has arisen between the USA and Yugoslavia over the **shooting down** of a US aircraft and the detention of its crew, when it was forced out of its way over Yugoslav territory by a storm.

10 Saturday

Housewives who like to save their fat ration by buying liquid paraffin to make cakes, are causing a shortage at chemist's shops and holding up the dispensing of medical prescriptions.

■ An Englishwoman, Mrs Burr (72), wins the women's title at the World **Archery** Championships in Stockholm, Sweden.

■ 10,843,164 **tons of rain** 2.11ins – falls on Birmingham in 19hrs. It is the city's second wettest day since 1891 (see pages 66-67).

11 Sunday

British actor **David Niven** returns to Scotland this month to play the lead in the film *Bonnie Prince Charlie*, with **Margaret Leighton** (pictured above with director Alex Korda). A famous Edinburgh firm of kiltmakers has been busy for weeks weaving special tartans of 1745.

■ Britain will import 1,200 tons of hothouse **grapes,** 200 tons of peaches and 500 tons of onions from Belgium between this October and July next year.

12 Monday
Full Moon

A trunk containing **Mussolini's body**, which was stolen from its grave in Milan in April, is delivered to Milan's Chief of Police by a Franciscan friar.

■ More than 200 **Colorado beetles**,

BIRTH OF THE UNITED NATIONS

Until the beginning of 1946, the United Nations existed only as the UN Charter, which had been drawn up at the San Franciso Conference in 1945. 1946 is the year it really begins. It is made up as follows:

THE GENERAL ASSEMBLY
Delegates of 51 nations. It convenes for the first time in London in January 1946 and quickly establishes:
The Security Council 11 members, 5 of which are the Great Powers (USA, USSR, UK, France and China) plus 6 who sit for 2 years at a time, and responsible for world security.
Atomic Energy Commission to monitor the development of nuclear energy and in particular its use as an aggressive force.
The following UN organisations are also set up this year:
ILO	International Labour Organisation
FAO	Food and Agriculture Organisation
WHO	World Health Organisation
UNESCO	United Nations Educational, Scientific and Cultural Organisation

AUGUST

destroyers of potato crops, have been removed from one potato field at Wallington, nr Kings Lynn, Norfolk. They probably came to the UK from America in ships' cargoes.

13 Tuesday

The King (below) is to deliver a message to the nation, designed to mobilise public opinion in support of the UN (see panel, facing page) and its work for world peace on September 29, to inaugurate United Nations Week.
... Six of the Rand's biggest goldmines have been brought to a standstill by a strike of 45,000 black South African mineworkers ...

14 Wednesday

Decrees nisi, made absolute today in the Divorce Courts under the new 6-week rule total 2,316, a record.
■ South African premier **General Smuts** says South Africa wants to see a European influx into the country that will re-create it.
■ Winston Churchill, Leader of the Opposition, is installed as Lord Warden and Admiral of the Cinque Ports at Dover, Kent.

15 Thursday

The yellow lights that illuminate the Bath Road at Harmondsworth, Middlesex are to be changed to blue in case pilots mistake the road for a lit-up London Airport runway which runs alongside it.
■ With the birth of her 17th child, Mrs Joseph McErlain of Toone, Northern Ireland draws a bigger **family allowance** than any other mother in Britain. She collects £3.5s per week for her 13 eligible children.
■ The Italian Government arranges for the **re-burial** of Mussolini's body in a secret place after the corpse's macabre movements during the last 4 months.

H G WELLS DIES

Dateline: August 12
H G Wells, author of such notable books as *The War of the Worlds*, **and** *The Time Machine*, dies at home in London on the eve of his 80th birthday. Author J B Priestley leads the tributes at his funeral, saying, 'at his worst he never hurt us, at his best he made us feel that we live on a star'.

16 Friday

A conference of **squatters** from all the camps in the Doncaster, Yorks, area is to be held to draw up health measures and codes of conduct. The squatters are taking over army and other camps as the servicemen move out.
■ The funeral of **H G Wells** takes place (see panel above).

17 Saturday

A **memorial** to 13 British commandos who made a suicide stand at Berneval, Normandy, while covering the Canadian raid on Dieppe in August 1942, is unveiled today in the presence of Mr Mackenzie King, the Canadian prime minister.
■ The film *Caesar and Cleopatra*, starring **Claude Rains** and **Vivien Leigh**, is sweeping the USA, and *Henry V* directed by and starring Laurence Olivier is in its 30th successful week in Boston.

18 Sunday

Forty-three people are killed and 57 injured when **mines** explode on a beach from which hundreds were bathing, near Pola, south of Trieste, Italy. The mines had been swept from the sea and were piled high on the beach awaiting disposal.
■ Under new corporation by-laws in Dublin, **cabbies** are reminded that they must not fall asleep on the roofs of their cabs.

69

AUGUST

19 Monday

More than 3,000 people have been killed in **Calcutta** after 3 days of fighting between Moslems and Hindus over Britain's plan for India's constitution. The Moslem minority wants to create its own state of Pakistan and insists on a split into two *(see July 29)*.
■ A Communist radio station in North China broadcasts orders to 130 million Chinese Communists to mobilise for a full-scale **civil war** to shatter the offensive of Chiang Kai-Shek's Nationalist forces.

20 Tuesday

Odette Sansom *(above)*, better known as 'Odette', has been awarded the **George Cross** for her 'courage, endurance and self-sacrifice'. While working with the French Resistance during the war, Odette was captured and tortured by the Gestapo but steadfastly refused to talk.
■ Professional footballers threaten to **strike** for a minimum wage of £7 per week.
■ A new case of **infantile paralysis** (poliomyelitis) is reported in London bringing the total to 14. There have been three deaths.

21 Wednesday

Princess Margaret is 16 today.
■ The American Government delivers a 48-hr ultimatum to Yugoslavia demanding the release of the Americans shot down in Yugoslavia and asking them to allow an investigation into the disappearance of a US Army plane nr Marshal Tito's summer home in Bled.
■ Partly because of the soaring birth-rate, **milk** supplies will be cut to two pints a week for non-priority consumers.
■ It is reported that 10,000 people in Hamburg, including doctors, are starving.

22 Thursday

600,000 Londoners will go without **milk** today because Co-op process workers are on strike for higher wages, and the strike is spreading to Kent, Norfolk and Suffolk.
■ The European Athletics Championship is opened in Oslo, Norway, by **King Haakon**. 30,000 people watch the march past.
■ Nine crew and passengers of the US plane **shot down** by Yugoslavia are released in Ljubljana this afternoon.
■ Paper losses in the **Wall Street** financial market's worst slump for 6yrs are estimated at more than $1,000 million (£250 million).

23 Friday

A plea for more **women police** officers to deal with problem dockland girls is made by the East Ham, London, probation officers in their annual report.
■ **Pandit Nehru** is appointed head of India's provisional government by the Viceroy, Lord Wavell.
■ At the European Athletics Championships in Oslo, Britain's **Sidney Wooderson**, 32, *(left)* wins the 5,000m in 14 mins 8.6 secs, and John Archer wins the 100m in 10.6secs.

24 Saturday

The **Waldorf Astoria** and 40 other hotels in New York have sacked their bands after the Musicians' Union demands more money. They say it makes dancing too costly.
■ Britain's athletes come **third** in the medals table at the European Athletics Championships in Oslo. Sweden is first and Finland is second.
■ 70,000 watch **England** draw 2-2 with Scotland in the Bolton Disaster Relief match at Manchester *(see March 9)*.

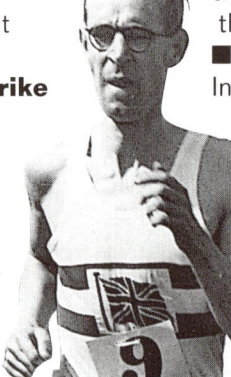

AUGUST

25 Sunday
New Moon

Despite government attempts to keep it in check, the **black market** in sweets, nylons and other luxury goods is flourishing in Britain, but food is fairly distributed. On the Continent, the poor have a struggle to survive as they cannot afford black market prices.
■ **Bing Crosby** (above), star of the current film hit *The Bells of St Mary's*, returns to American radio in October. He will be paid £7,500 a week, the highest salary ever paid to a radio star in the USA.

26 Monday

No sceptic of future ages will be able to pour cold water on the rare gifts of Ben, the **talking dog**. His voice has been recorded for posterity by the BBC, who sent a team of interviewers and engineers to Royston, Herts, to record Ben saying his famous phrase, 'I want one.'
■ Two of Britain's biggest box-office stars, **Phyllis Calvert** and **Ann Todd**, leave on the *Queen Mary* bound for Hollywood. Ann is to make *The Paradine Case* and Phyllis *Time Out of Mind*.

27 Tuesday

The resident representative of Britain's Ministry of Food in Denmark spends £1 million on 80,000 **cattle** and 7,000 tons of cheese for the British zone of Germany.
■ The Italian Government says no to a US government request that it should grant temporary hospitality to 25,000 **Jewish refugees**, mostly from Poland. Italy has its own refugee problem as thousands of Italians have fled Venezia Giulia, fearing they will soon come under Yugoslav control.

28 Wednesday

A call for a halt in the daily rise of the cost of living in the USA comes from two million workers. The Confederated Unions of America telegraph **President Truman**, urging him to recall Congress to amend the Price Laws.
■ Two degrees of **frost** is recorded in Birmingham – the first August frost there since 1938 – and gales bring havoc to the south coast, causing floods and damage to houses *(see pages 66-67)*.
■ **George Bernard Shaw**, famed Irish playwright of such classics as *Pygmalion*, *St Joan* and *Man & Superman*, has become an Honorary Freeman of Dublin, the city of his birth. He signs the Roll brought from Ireland for the occasion *(below)* at his home in Ayot St Lawrence, Herts. It's the first time Dublin's Roll of Freemen has left the city.

29 Thursday

Walt Disney has given permission for a stage adaptation of his *Snow White and the Seven Dwarfs* to be produced in London. It opens in Wimbledon on September 2, before moving to the West End for Christmas.

SEPTEMBER

■ Sweden, Iceland and Afghanistan have been accepted into membership of the United Nations. Albania, Outer Mongolia, Eire, Transjordan and Portugal are rejected.

30 Friday

Six hundred people a day are enquiring in London about **emigrating** to one of the Dominions.

■ Gabriel Pascal has sold the contract of **Deborah Kerr**, 25 (*below*), star of such films as *Major Barbara, Love on the Dole* and *Perfect Strangers*, to Hollywood's MGM for $200,000. Miss Kerr gets a guaranteed weekly salary of $3,000 for 5yrs whether she makes a film or not.

31 Saturday

Fifty people are **killed** and 200 injured in Bombay when riots break out between Hindus and Moslems on the eve of the first all-Indian Interim Government taking office. A state of emergency is declared and a curfew is imposed (*see July 29 and Aug 19*).

■ **Jitterbugging** takes over Bath. The Bath Spa Committee is considering appointing a master of ceremonies to control jitterbugging at its winter dances after receiving many complaints about the jitterbuggers spoiling Pavilion dances for hundreds of other people.

... The wettest and coldest August for 5yrs ends with floods in Yorkshire and swirling showers over the rest of Britain ...

SEPTEMBER

1 Sunday

A **referendum** in Greece overwhelmingly approves the restoration of the monarchy. The Greek government declares that it will punish anyone who is disrespectful to the king or the monarchy.

■ **Marshal Tito** sends a note to the US government expressing regret over the shooting down of American planes over Yugoslavia (*see Aug 21*).

2 Monday

Evidence that Japan is determined to **rebuild** her shattered economy is provided by the 5-Year Plan launched today. It outlines plans for the reorganisation and redistribution of industry, the restoration of its devastated cities, and the reduction of unemployment.

■ **Charlie Chaplin** (57) is throwing away his famous moustache, bowler hat and walking stick. His new film, *Monsieur Verdoux*, is based on the exploits of the French bluebeard Landru, in which Chaplin murders 18 women for their money.

3 Tuesday

There will be fewer King Edwards, London's favourite **potato**, on sale this winter because of the blight.

■ Italy gets Britain's war **reparations** bill – a total of £2,888 million, of which £29 million is for damage to the island of Malta.

■ 7,000 British servicemen in Germany are seeking permission for their wives and children to join them, causing some **discontent** among the Germans who are dispossessed of their houses as a result.

4 Wednesday

The first Royal Command Film Performance will take place on November 1 at the Empire Theatre, Leicester Square, London. It will be attended by the King, the Queen and the two Princesses. The programme includes the premiere of a new film, and a 1hr stage show.

■ **Eagles** attack a Turkish aeroplane over the Taurus mountains, causing it to make a forced landing.

... A walk-out by 100,000 American seamen may delay today's sailing of the *Queen Mary* for New York ...

SEPTEMBER

5 Thursday

Football: Nottingham Forest offer Hibernian £10,000 for the Scots international winger, Gordon Smith, but it is rejected.
■ More than 100,000 tons of **cereals** and cereal products bound for Europe is held up in US ports by the seamen's strike.
. . . London's meat and milk STRIKES end today . . .

6 Friday

The Ministry of Health is to regulate the sale of **ice cream**. This summer, one barrel at Aberystwyth caused 140 people to fall ill and 4 to die of typhoid fever.
■ Two thousand French **patriots** are presented with a certificate signed by Gen Eisenhower and Air Marshal Lord Tedder, by the British and American ambassadors to France. During the occupation more than 5,000 British, Canadian, and US servicemen were returned to liberty, thanks to their devotion and that of thousands of other French people at risk of torture and death.
■ The citizens of the American town of Henrietta, Texas, are put on their **honour** to be law-abiding by the mayor, because the 7-strong police force is striking for more pay.

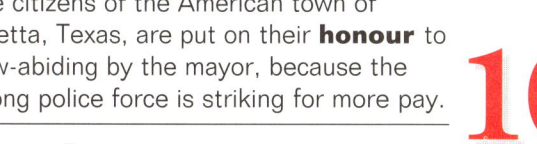

7 Saturday

Two RAF Meteors based at Tangmere, Sussex, set a new World Air Speed Record with a speed of 614mph. The previous record was 606¼mph.
■ Because the King cannot attend the London **premier** of the Battle of Arnhem film *Theirs is the Glory* on September 17, he has commanded a private showing for the Queen and himself at Balmoral.

8 Sunday

One thousand **squatters**, organised by the Communist Party, seize flats and houses in London's West End *(see panel, pages 74-75)*.
■ The *New York Times* reports that **Princess Elizabeth** is likely to become engaged to her second cousin, **Prince Philip** of Greece, a rumour denied by Buckingham Palace. Prince Philip is currently a guest at Balmoral, and today attends the service at Crathie Church.
■ As **flood reports** pour in from all over the country, harvest festival services, which normally celebrate the safe gathering in of the harvest, are changed, and prayers are said for better weather.

9 Monday

The government will not support the **squatters** who seized the block of luxury flats and other buildings yesterday. The owners will be able to exercise their full legal rights to reclaim their property.
■ A Roman bathroom with a pink concrete floor and a living room with a red-tessellated pavement are the latest treasures uncovered on the site of a Canterbury, Kent, hotel destroyed by the Blitz in 1942.

10 Tuesday

The **Palestine Conference** opens in London with representatives from 7 Arab states but no Palestinian Arabs, and no Jewish representatives either from Palestine or outside.
■ Australia has given the go ahead to British shipping companies to carry up to 70,000 **immigrants** a year for the next 10yrs, but the ships' capacity is limited to just 30,000 people next year.
■ **Lord Nuffield** *(above)* gives £10,000 to the Army Benevolent Fund, which is appealing for £1,000,000.
A 4½lb conger eel is caught in the main street of Newry, Co Down. The nearest river is a mile away.

SEPTEMBER

11 Wednesday
Full Moon

Ben Smith MP, the former Minister of Food, is leaving politics to accept a post with the National Coal Board in the Midlands.
■ The film *Caesar and Cleopatra* is smashing the house record at Broadway's Astor Theatre, New York. It took £2,800 on the first day, beating the figures of such outstanding successes as *Spellbound*, starring Ingrid Bergman and Gregory Peck, and Danny Kaye's *The Kid from Brooklyn*.
■ Mr Ferguson's *Airborne*, ridden by T Lowrey, follows up his Derby victory by winning the St Leger.

12 Thursday

The government announces the repatriation of 15,000 **German POWs** a month. About 394,000 are eligible to go, but not senior officers or those known to be strongly pro-Nazi.
■ An Oxford **degree** with first-class honours is worth only 5s.9d. a week in the teaching profession, Mr W Parkinson, head of Bridlington School, Yorks, tells his boys on speech day.

13 Friday

Nearly 2 million New Yorkers are out of work because of the lorry drivers' and seamen's **strikes**.
■ A Berlin jeweller gives the Americans the first clue to the whereabouts of the German Reich's **hidden treasures** in return for his wife being brought back to him from S Germany – about £37.5 million has been found this week.

14 Saturday

Five prominent members of the British **Communist Party** are arrested on a charge of conspiring to incite and direct trespass. Minister of Health, Aneurin Bevan, writes a letter to all local authorities asking them to withhold all facilities, especially gas or electricity, from any squatters entering property under their control.

HOME IS A SUITCASE AT THE END OF THE BED

HOMELESSNESS in the wake of the war is a major public issue, with the the demand for housing outstripping supply amid a big rebuilding programme. Some people take matters into their own hands, by squatting in empty premises. Baby Patricia Mullins *(right)* sleeps in a makeshift cot – a suitcase – while her 32-year-old mum feeds her brother and sister in Duchess of Bedford House, Kensington, in one of 46 flats occupied by squatters. *Below left:* **A woman is arrested trying to deliver food to squatters at Abbey Lodge, Regent's Park;** *Below centre:* **Sightseers are intrigued by washing day at Duchess of Bedford House;** *Below right:* **A man arrested for obstruction outside the squatter-occupied Ivanhoe Hotel, Bloomsbury.**

SEPTEMBER

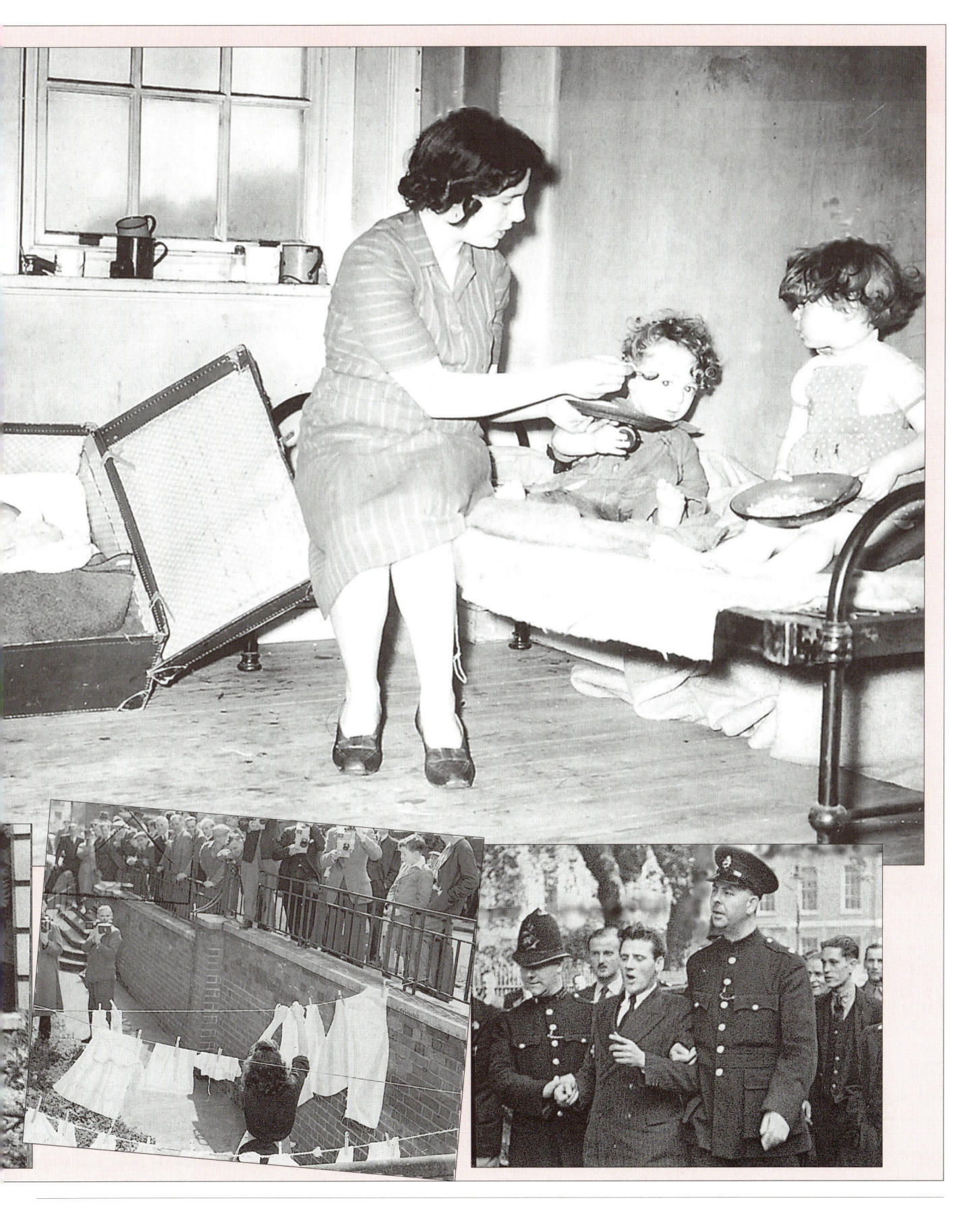

75

SEPTEMBER

■ **Skyscrapers** are on their way out, according to US architects who now consider that they look good, help the skyline, but don't pay their way.

15 Sunday

Hollywood embarks on a major economy drive. Feature players, producers and directors are sacked, and hundreds more face losing their jobs. There has been no suggestion that senior executives like **Louis B Mayer**, who gets £250,000 a year, should take a salary cut.

. . . The number of casualties in the communal **RIOTS** in Bombay since the beginning of the month total 262 dead and 795 injured . . .

16 Monday

President Truman asks the United Nations to summon a world scientific conference to study global resources, including the possible peaceful uses of atomic energy.

■ **Larry Adler**, the American harmonica player whose fan clubs in Britain claim more than 300,000 members, all harmonica players, is to tour Britain in October.

■ 4,000 New York **barbers** stage a walk-out for higher wages.

. . . The Russian chess team beats a team from the USA by 12½ games to 7½ games in their match in Moscow . . .

17 Tuesday

Five hundred **squatters** leave the Duchess of Bedford House, Kensington, following the court's decision that they must leave within three days.

■ **Bruce Woodcock**, the British Heavyweight Champion, knocks out Gus Lesnovich (USA) in the 8th round of their contest at Harringay Arena, London.

18 Wednesday

The War Office drafts in a fleet of 4-wheel 'go anywhere' vehicles, complete with cranes, to help farmers in Suffolk lift the crops off wet and soggy land.

■ The Players' Union, which has been given a mandate by 2,000 British footballers to take any action necessary over the demand for increased **wages**, tells the Football League management that their members want an increase from £10 to £12 a week in season and from £8 to £10 a week during the summer.

. . . JOE LOUIS, the US heavyweight champion, collects $33,506 for 2min 9sec work when he knocks out Tami Mauriello (USA) . . .

19 Thursday

In a speech in Switzerland, which is broadcast worldwide, former premier **Winston Churchill** calls for a 'united

---

CARTOON FUN . . . WITH DAN DOOFER

SEPTEMBER

states of Europe to ensure future peace', and says that the reconciliation and partnership of France and Germany is the first step.
■ Within 30hrs of its disappearance, a giant Belgian Skymaster airliner with 44 people on boards is spotted 25 miles south-west of Gander Airport, Newfoundland, Canada. Supplies are dropped in the hope that there are some survivors.
■ In Australia, pylons supporting **Sydney Harbour Bridge** are being used as dwellings by homeless people.

20 Friday

Five **survivors** of the Belgian Skymaster crash are reached by rescue parties *(see Sept 19)*.
■ The first **Cannes Film Festival**, which was meant to take place in 1939, opens in the south of France.
■ Factories, schools and shops in Yorkshire and Lancashire close as **flood waters** rise to maroon thousands in the upper rooms of houses, and sweep away sheep and cattle. (Barnsley under water, above – more pictures, pages 66-67).

21 Saturday

Warner Brothers signs **Humphrey Bogart** for another 15yrs without option. He will make one picture a year for a salary of £50,000. Bogart (47) star of such films as *High Sierra, The Maltese Falcon, Casablanca*, and later this year *The Big Sleep*, gets most of his fan mail from women.
■ Cities and towns all over the country report a great rush to enrol in night schools. Ex-servicemen are making evening classes a priority.
. . . The largest audience ever attends the LAST NIGHT OF THE PROMS in London's Albert Hall. Sir Adrian Boult directs the proceedings . . .

22 Sunday

So many **new babies** are expected in the areas to which wives of BAOR soldiers are going, that a special district nurse service has been organised in Germany.
■ Frankfurt, Germany, the original home of the Rothschilds, has restored its synagogue, and it will reopen next Thursday, the Jewish New Year.
. . . Two million Italians are unemployed – one in 20 of the working population . . .

23 Monday

The **Faroe Islands**, 200 miles north of the Orkneys and ruled by Denmark since 1300, declare their independence.
■ **Paul Robeson**, the famous American negro singer and actor who heads a crusade against lynching, warns President Truman that if the government does not act to stop the lynching of negroes, the negroes will.
■ **General Eisenhower**, the US Chief of the General Staff, leaves Halifax, Nova Scotia, on the *Queen Mary*, to inspect US occupation forces in Europe.

24 Tuesday

Nearly 200,000 Jews go on **strike** in Tel Aviv, Palestine, for 3hrs in protest against the alleged murder of a Jew when 900 illegal immigrants tried to run the blockade of British ships in Haifa, and one fell overboard and drowned.
■ The King opens the 'Britain Can Make It' exhibition at the Victoria and Albert Museum, organised by the Council of Industrial Design.
■ **Bad weather** during August means that

SEPTEMBER

only 61,000 tons of the wheat crop was harvested instead of the expected 75,000 tons.

25 Wednesday
New Moon

Civil war threatens Greece as fighting continues between the monarchist government troops and the opposition (republican) forces.
■ The London Philharmonic Orchestra plays to an audience of 300 people in Shoreditch Town Hall, London. The **concert** is organised by the National Union of Tailors and Garment Workers as part of a drive to get more workers for the industry.
■ **Shannon**, the Wembley-trained greyhound, sets a new track record in the final of the Thames Silver Salver at Southend, Essex, with a time of 27.89sec.

26 Thursday
Dominion Day, New Zealand

At the end of his trial for murder at the Old Bailey, ex-Borstal boy and 'charmer' **Neville George Clovely Heath** (above) is found guilty of the murder of his first victim, Mrs Margery Gardner. The other charge, the murder of Doreen Marshall, is not proceeded with, but mentioned by the Prosecution. He is sentenced to be hanged at Pentonville Prison on October 16.
. . . Americans spent £164,750,000 on cosmetics last year . . .

27 Friday

Pravda newspaper, the organ of Russia's Central Committee, attacks Moscow theatres for putting on plays by British novelist and playwright **W Somerset Maugham**, saying they are typical examples of bourgeois salons. It adds that J B Priestley's *They Came to the City* is showing in 68 Soviet theatres, and George Bernard Shaw's *Pygmalion* in 30 venues.

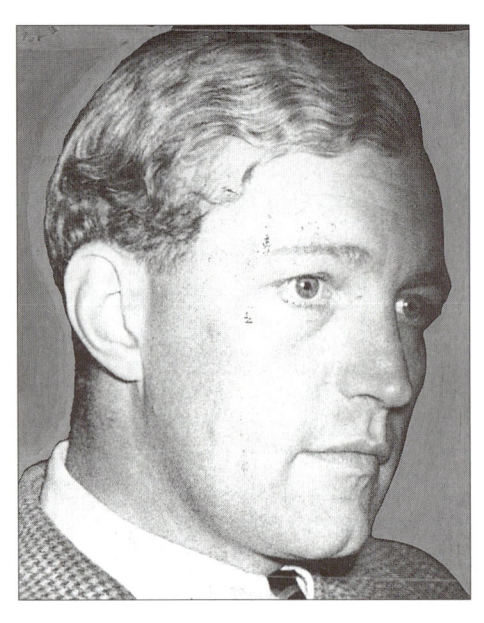

28 Saturday

Following *Pravda's* comments on **W Somerset Maugham**, the Moscow newspaper, *Vechernaya Moskva* attacks Russian publishers for re-issuing the Sherlock Holmes stories as Holmes's character is 'dangerous to Soviet morals and ideologies – diverting attention from the social contradictions of capitalist reality'.
■ Doctors and nurses are working day and night to prevent an **epidemic** starting among the 15,000 victims of the Salford, Lancashire, floods. As the water recedes, rats are invading houses, together with a mass invasion of beetles.

29 Sunday

United Nations week. More than 1,000 events are planned all over the country, including cathedral services, floodlight processions, concerts, firework displays and mass demonstrations to encourage the British to show their interest in peace.
■ According to the president of the National Hairdressers and Cosmetologist Association's convention in Chicago, USA, glamour girls are out of date, and in their place is coming the demure girl who can boil an egg as well as she can jitterbug.
. . . The 11.30pm-4.30am curfew on Berliners in the British zone is to be lifted on October 6 . . .

30 Monday

Six '**Goldwyn Girls**' – hand-picked lovelies – have arrived in Britain to show off US fashions. They have brought 61 suitcases of sportswear, cocktail dresses, afternoon and evening gowns to dazzle British eyes, but only 3 pairs of nylons each. Top British mannequins are leaving shortly for the USA to show off the latest British fashions.
■ The Nuremberg **War Crimes** Tribunal begins to deliver its judgements.

OCTOBER

FAMOUS TEST PILOT DISAPPEARS

SEP 27 Test pilot Geoffrey de Havilland fails to return from a test flight over Hatfield, Herts, in the *Swallow* (below) – the high-speed tail-less jet-propelled plane in which he hoped to attack the world air speed record. His body is washed ashore at Whitstable, Kent, 10 days later.

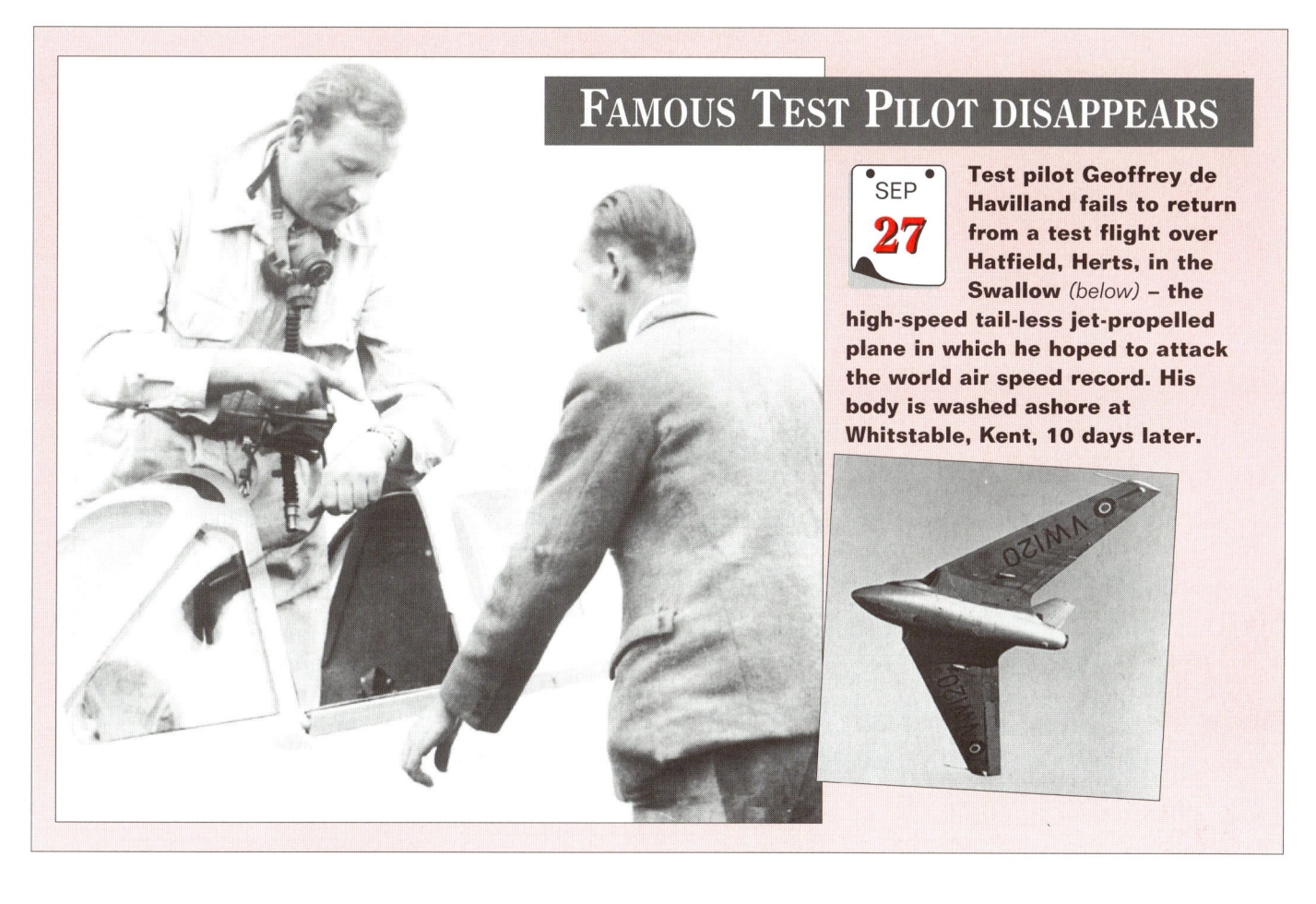

OCTOBER

1 Tuesday

■ The final stages of the **Nuremberg Trials** in Germany are broadcast on the BBC Light programme *(see page 87)*.
■ The first major delivery of **goat meat** is on its way to Britain from New Zealand on the *Ozani*. Until now small quantities have been used in meat pies.

2 Wednesday

At the International Conference of Tourist Organisations in Britain, Lord Inman, Principal Adviser on **tourism** to the Board of Trade, says Britain will actively seek tourists and visas will be freely granted next year.
■ American singer and film star **Grace Moore**, who is in Britain for a series of concerts, stuns her audiences with a dazzling dress. Of billowing white, it is decorated with tiny gold bars of music from all the operas she has sung, and has the melodies from her first film *One Night of Love*, across her shoulders.
■ At a medical symposium at the University of Buffalo, New York, Dr William Reinkoff poses the theory that smoking may be allied to **lung cancer**.

3 Thursday

The first annual **conference** of the Conservative party to be held since 1937 opens in Blackpool.
■ The Musicians Union orders its members not to play on board the *Queen Elizabeth*, due to make her first trial run this weekend from the Clyde to Southampton with the Queen and the two Princesses on board. The Union claims that the musicians are being offered £23 a month – the same pay as assistant stewards.

79

OCTOBER

4 Friday

President Truman reiterates his demand that Britain should admit 100,000 Jewish displaced persons to Palestine. Arab leaders warn that the aggressive US policy over Jewish immigration could lead to a revocation of all Middle East oil concessions and the severance of diplomatic relations.
■ Mr Attlee reshuffles his **Cabinet**. Among the new appointments, A V Alexander is appointed to the new post of Defence Minister; P Noel Baker replaces Lord Stansgate as Secretary of State for Air; his own place as Minister of State is taken by **Hector McNeil** (below); Lord Nathan becomes Minister for Civil Aviation, and Mr Bellenger becomes Secretary of State for War.

5 Saturday

Kent **farmers** are asking children to collect nuts to supplement feeding supplies and offer them 5s. a cwt for acorns and 7s.6d. a cwt for beech nuts.
■ Screen stars **Myrna Loy** and **Orson Welles** are each demanding damages of £250,000 from Matthew Woll, the vice-president of the American Federation of Labour, alleging that he described them as Communists.

6 Sunday

The RAF **Comforts** Committee reports that during the war and up to the end of April it had received £152,452 in cash, and 'comforts' worth £7,200,000, which include 61,667 dartboards, 29,336 domino sets, 340,988 packs of cards, 9,610 footballs, 22,942 radios, 8,335 gramophones, 160,044,794 packs of cigarettes and 428 pianos.
■ Britain's **lifeboats** were launched 63 times last month – one more launching than during the Battle of Britain in September 1940.
■ Old English **mastiffs** are to be imported from the USA as the breed is dying out here.

7 Monday

The body of **Geoffrey de Havilland** is washed ashore at Whitstable, Kent. *(See panel, page 79)*.
■ Col Frank Hanley, US Military Governor of Berlin, warns that TB in the city has reached epidemic proportions.

8 Tuesday

Four of London's luxury hotels, the Savoy, Claridges, the Berkeley and the Dorchester, are hit by the **catering workers' strike** for union recognition. The strike is beginning to spread to top-class restaurants as well.
■ **Driving tests** will recommence on November 1. Nearly 750,000 are still driving on provisional licences.

9 Wednesday

Happy Birthday: The Duke of Kent is 11.
■ Fifteen people are killed and 119 injured when 30,000 strikers and unemployed **riot** in Rome over unemployment, lack of housing and the high cost of living.
■ The Royal Observatory, Greenwich, forecasts a thrilling display from 8.30pm onwards tonight when the **comet** Giacobini-Zinner will be throwing off luminous particles at the rate of 500 a minute.
■ According to British United Press, 20% of all the babies born in Munich in August were illegitimate.

80

OCTOBER

10 Thursday
Full Moon

China is officially on a **war** footing. The Nationalist Government in Nanking re-imposes military rule in the country and all male Chinese between the ages of 18-45 are liable for military service.
■ Health Minister **Aneurin Bevan** tells parliament that there are 39,535 squatters occupying 1,038 ex-service camps in England and Wales, which cannot therefore be released for housing, and they will have to be moved.
■ The **War Crimes** Tribunal in Nuremburg rejects the pleas for clemency from 11 of the 12 Nazis sentenced to death (see page 87).

11 Friday

The **Duke and Duchess of Windsor** arrive in England. It is the first visit the Duchess has made to this country since she left it 10yrs ago as Mrs Wallis Simpson, and the Duke, then King Edward VIII, abdicated the throne to marry the woman he loved.
■ In an address to the Dutch Parliament at the Hague, South African premier Field Marshal **Jan Smuts** (above) calls on Britain to take the lead in forming a United States of Europe.
■ Prime Minister Attlee is invested as a Knight of the Order of St John of Jerusalem.

12 Saturday

Italian MPs are complaining about actress **Sarah Churchill** (daughter of Winston Churchill, Leader of the Opposition), who with a crowd of extras is being filmed in Rome's parliament building for a new picture. The MPs are reported to be shocked to find themselves mingling with **fake MPs.**
■ Twenty military **prisoners** in Dartmoor go on strike in an attempt to get their sentences reviewed.

13 Sunday

Remedies used aboard ships in the 18th century, such as the burning of **feathers** to revive a fainting fit, are still included in the new edition of *The Ship's Captain's Medical Guide*, published by the Ministry of War.
■ When the National Association of Girls Clubs ask 6,000 of their members to name their favourite pastime, **dancing** is the answer – even above going to the cinema.
■ Nine out of 10 undergraduate **students** at Oxford and Cambridge are ex-servicemen.

14 Monday

Magistrates at Burnham, Bucks, have a **whip-round** among themselves to pay the fare back to London of a man they have just bound over for larceny.
■ The Thames Conservancy Board raises no objection to the mooring of ex-navy landing craft to use as houseboats, provided the necessary regulations are obeyed.
■ Britain is back to producing golf balls – 10 million this year – a third of the world's total.

. . . 6.5million EGGS arrive in London from Australia . .

15 Tuesday

The Paris **Peace Conference** ends. The 21 nations attending approve draft treaties with Finland, Bulgaria, Rumania, Hungary and Italy for consideration by the Foreign Ministers of the **Big Four** (UK, USA, USSR, France), who will begin writing the final treaties in New York on November 4.
■ All but 30 of the 315 military prisoners in Dartmoor prison are now on hunger strike, demanding revision of their sentences.

16 Wednesday

Ten Nazi **war criminals** are hanged in the prison gymnasium at Nuremberg. (See panel, page 87).
■ Mr Justice Evershed reverses the decision

OCTOBER

of the Register of Trade Marks and decides to allow an American **footwear** company to register the word 'Oomphies' as their trade mark in Britain. He says there is no salacious or improper significance in applying the word to women's footwear.

17 Thursday

From November 1, **L-plates** will again make their appearance on cars driven by learners. The learner driver will also have to be accompanied by an experienced driver. Those who have held a provisional licence for over a year will be exempt from taking the driving test.

■ £34,000 in **cash** is found in the pockets of used clothing given to UNRRA by Americans for distribution to needy Italians.

. . . At least 5,000 people have died in the Hindu v Muslim riots in Bengal, India, since last Thursday . . .

18 Friday

The City of New York offers the **United Nations** a 350-acre site at Flushing Meadow, Queens, as its permanent home.

■ In a broadcast on American radio, the US Secretary of State, James Byrnes, admits he is disturbed by the 'continued, if not increasing, tension between the USA and the USSR'.

■ A burial urn, in a wonderful state of preservation, and containing calcified human **remains**, is unearthed at the Kirk Ireton quarries in Derbyshire. It may date from 1500BC.

19 Saturday

In a £1 million share deal, American film giants **Warner Brothers** and **Metro-Goldwyn-Mayer** win control of British Associated Pictures' 600 cinema theatres and, thus, film distribution in Britain.

■ One peppercorn a year is all the rent asked by the Marquess of Northampton's Trust for the lease of land needed for improving Islington's public gardens.

■ An unofficial strike of busmen seriously affects the travel of 20,000 miners to the pits of S Wales and Monmouthshire.

20 Sunday

Summer temperatures bring the crowds to the beaches in the south east, while an 80-mile-long blanket of fog stretches along the E Yorkshire coast.

■ The Chinese Nationalist Government persuades Communist leader **Chou en Lai** to visit Nanking and resume peace talks. It is feared that China is on the brink of famine, caused by the civil war, the flooding of more than 500,000 acres by the Yellow River and a plague of **locusts** destroying the crops.

. . . In Germany, Berliners go to the polls for the city's first free elections in 14 years . . .

21 Monday

Crowds cheer, cranes dip in salute, sirens sound and the fireboats spray fountains of water when the liner *Queen Elizabeth* arrives in New York. Her crossing time is 4 days, 10hrs 18mins.

■ Eleven out of 19 **bombed churches** in the City of London, amongst them *St Mary le Bow* (Bow Bells) are to be rebuilt.

■ The 78th Annual Conference of the **TUC** opens in Brighton, Sussex. Membership of affiliated trades unions now stands at a record 6,671,120.

22 Tuesday

Foreign Secretary **Ernest Bevin** (*pictured, left*) tells the House of Commons that the British Government has worked out a plan by which German heavy industry will be owned and worked by the German people, but be subject to international control.

OCTOBER

A GRAND OLD LADY BACK IN SERVICE

OCT 8

SHE'S BACK ... The Queen Elizabeth, newly-converted from troopship to luxury liner in the King George V Dry Dock at Southampton, where she is pictured in August, is ready to go back into passenger service. After the refit, the Queen takes the wheel of the liner while sailing at 30 knots during speed trials off Arran, Scotland. 'It was so easy to handle, I was surprised,' the Queen said.

23 Wednesday

■ Five great bronze chandeliers with 400 candleholders, saved from the **fire** which burned down the House of Commons in 1834, will be used in the new House when rebuilding (after the Blitz) is completed.

■ To combat the **shortage of nurses**, a Birmingham hospital is sending two ward sisters to Ireland to recruit 'jolly Irish girls with laughing eyes'.

In his speech at the opening of the second meeting of the **UN Assembly** at Flushing Meadow, New York, President Truman warns the delegates that disaster will strike the world if the UN splits into two political groups.

■ Objecting to the word '**fathercraft**' in a report recommending courses for fathers at evening institutes, as 'we must uphold the dignity of the head of the family', Alderman Mrs N C Rye tells the LCC education committee that she agrees to the substitution of 'parentcraft' or 'housecraft'.

24 Thursday
New Moon

The Ministry of Food declares that Britain's ports will be open to take practically all the **fruit** that overseas countries can send us at reasonable prices.

83

OCTOBER

■ Chicago packing **heiress**, Mrs Lewis Swift Jr – an ex-circus bareback rider – raises a storm of protest from American animal lovers when she allows a pig to be used as an obstacle by 30 riders who jumped over it on her estate. 'It's preposterous,' she says. 'The pig wasn't hurt and was merely used as scenery.'

25 Friday

The Soviets are reported to be dismantling German **arms factories** and taking them to the USSR, where they are being reassembled. Earlier this week Reuters reported that electrical engineers in the Russian sector of Berlin are being rounded up and sent eastwards with their families.

■ 6,000 **busmen** return to work in S Wales and the border counties. The 14-day strike caused a loss of 15,000 tons of coal because miners were unable to travel to their pits.

26 Saturday

The King, Queen and the young princesses attend a **wedding** (see panel right).

■ Mount Klyuchi in Siberia, said to be the largest **volcano** in Europe or Asia, erupts.

27 Sunday

Moscow Dynamos, the crack Soviet soccer side, who had such a successful tour in Britain last year, are in deep trouble at home. A communist newspaper in Leningrad accuses them of 'hooliganism and conduct unbecoming gentlemen' on the football pitch.

■ Edward Carroll of Co Clare, Eire, was sued for breach of promise in the Galway Circuit Court, where some of his endearing letters were read out. One of them ended 'The higher the mountain, the cooler the breeze. The oftener we meet, the tighter the squeeze.' He was acquitted.

28 Monday

Soviet leader **Stalin** denies Winston Churchill's allegation (in the House of Commons on October 23) that Russia has 200 divisions on a war footing between the Baltic and Vienna, and Vienna and the Black Sea.

■ The threatened strike of 112 **mayors** in France's wine-growing Gerauld department, against government plans to freeze wine prices, has been called off after an appeal to the mayors by the president, M Bidault.

29 Tuesday

Soviet Foreign Minister **Molotov** puts a resolution before the UN General Assembly proposing general disarmament, and the prohibition of the production of atomic bombs for war purposes.

■ **Hugh Dalton**, Chancellor of the Exchequer, says 42,000 typewriters, 15,450 adding machines and 20,300 duplicating machines are in use in British government departments.

NOVEMBER

Princess Elizabeth, Princess Margaret and Princess Alexandra of Kent are bridesmaids to Lord Mountbatten's daughter, Pamela, when she marries Lord Brabourne at Romsey Abbey, Hants. The King, Queen and Prince Phillip of Greece are also among the guests.

PRINCESSES STEP OUT AS BRIDESMAIDS

30 Wednesday

- The British Embassy in Rome is wrecked by 2 explosions, thought to be the handiwork of Jewish terrorists.
- The USA backs Russia's proposal at the UN General Assembly in New York for immediate action on disarmament with safeguards.

31 Thursday

The Board of Trade says that the most that can be granted to a couple setting up house is 2 blankets and 3 sheets for each bed in use, but that quantities of Government surplus blankets should soon be available in the shops.
- The Oxford Union carries a motion that 'this house deplores the growing menace of **trade union tyranny**', by 255 votes to 121.

NOVEMBER

1 Friday

Thousands of people jam Leicester Square to see the King and Queen arrive for the first Royal Command Film Performance at the Empire Cinema: the crowds are so dense that the **King and Queen** are 12min late. Film stars are marooned in the vast crowd. First-aid men treat 100 people on the spot, and 3 people are taken to hospital with fractured legs. The film is *A Matter of Life and Death* starring David Niven and Roger Livesey.

2 Saturday

The Federation of Business and Professional Women's Clubs is sponsoring candidates for seats in local and national government in a fight for a share in national and international affairs. They are also training women from all walks of life to appreciate their own importance in public matters.
- Japan is showing an increased appetite for western music of all kinds, particularly opera, ballet and the symphony.

3 Sunday

In Spain, Franco's government arrests left-wing opponents to 'forestall a plot to launch a general uprising' to coincide with the UN's debate on Spain.
- A 10,000-strong crowd throws tomatoes and stones at mounted police in Trieste, Italy, at a demonstration to commemorate the 20th anniversary of the liberation of the city from the Austrians.

4 Monday

Peace talks between the Football League and the Players' Union result in an agreement on a minimum wage of £7 per week in winter and £5 per week in summer.
- **Beniamino Gigli**, the world's greatest tenor, returns to the Royal Opera House Covent Garden to sing Rodolfo in Puccini's *La Boheme*. Queen Mary, the Princess Royal and the Duchess of Kent are in the audience.

NOVEMBER

5 Tuesday

Fish and chip shop owners in many Lancashire towns are warned by the Food Office that, while there is no law against it, their refusal to sell **chips** without fish is considered unsatisfactory and unfair.
■ All London road and rail **fares** will go up on January 1. All 2d. fares will go up to 2½d. but the existing 1½d. fare remains unchanged.

6 Wednesday

The Royal Commission on Equal Pay says that women in industry should be paid less well than men, because they are less capable in a crisis. But they agree that in teaching, the Civil Service, the Post Office and local government equal pay may be advisable.
■ The **Republicans** sweep to power for the first time in 15yrs in the US elections.
... More than 1.5 million boxes of grapefruit and jaffa oranges are to be shipped from Palestine to reach the UK in time for Christmas ...

7 Thursday

The US Migration Service says that 12,000 marriages contracted between US soldiers and women they met abroad have already broken up. It also reports that some wives have arrived in the USA to find that their husband is at no known address, or is already married.

8 Friday

As a tribute to the **courage** of Londoners during the war, New Zealand will panel and furnish a room in London's new Guildhall, replacing the one destroyed by the Luftwaffe.
■ Foreign Secretary **Ernest Bevin** warns the US Secretary of State James Byrnes that there could be severe political repercussions in Germany because of the impending food crisis in the British zone.
■ The engagement is announced between **Mary Churchill**, youngest daughter of Opposition Leader Winston Churchill, and Coldstream Guards' Capt. Christopher Soames, whom she met only a month ago.

9 Saturday
Full Moon

Prime Minister Attlee, Field Marshal Lord Montgomery, War Minister Mr Bellinger and Foreign Secretary Ernest Bevin will receive special **police protection**, following death threats from Jewish terrorists.
■ The **Lockheed Constellation**, the biggest passenger-carrying plane in the world, which can take up to 168 passengers, makes its maiden flight in California, USA.

10 Sunday
Remembrance Sunday

The King unveils the plaque bearing the new inscription MCMXXXIX-MCMXLV (1939-1945) on the Cenotaph in Whitehall.
■ **Music lovers** attending symphony concerts of the Northern Philharmonic Orchestra in Leeds Town Hall complain about the odours seeping into the concert hall from the restaurant below, but it has had no effect on the attendance.

11 Monday

Traffic grinds to a halt, women are trampled underfoot, and scores of people faint as a crowd of 20,000 surge through the streets to

NOVEMBER

WAR CRIMINALS SENTENCED TO DEATH

DATELINE: October 1. The eyes of the world are on a Nuremberg courtroom, where 12 top Nazis, including Goering and von Ribbentrop, are sentenced to death. Another five are jailed and three are acquitted.
Rudolf Hess is jailed for life. Ten are hanged on October 16 in the prison gymnasium at Nuremberg. Hermann Goering commits suicide with a smuggled cyanide pellet just hours before he is due to be executed and Martin Bormann, who was sentenced to death in his absence, has so far evaded capture.

welcome ukulele-playing comedian **George Formby** (facing page) when he arrives in Cape Town, South Africa.

■ The UK's first 2 permanent British Iron & Steel Federation steel houses open at Grantham, Lincs. They are the forerunners of the 30,000 houses they will produce for the whole country.

■ **Ingrid Bergman** is voted the greatest box office star of 1946, just ahead of Bing Crosby, the most popular actor, in a nation-wide poll in the USA.

12 Tuesday

The Irish State Coach, followed by a Captain's escort of the Household Cavalry, takes the King and Queen to the Houses of Parliament where the King opens the new session. Special precautions are taken against possible action by Jewish terrorists.

■ The British Colour Council is hoping to cheer up **men's clothes** by sponsoring new colours. The range they suggest is Blue Grass Storm; Pacific Green; Catkin Cravat, Cream Batswing, and a selection of grey-blues - Sloeberry, Shell Grey, Smoke Haze, and Heather Blue.

13 Wednesday

500 tons of **grain** arrives in the British zone of Germany. It is the first delivery of 100,000 tons to be sent from the Russian zone under a new barter pact which came into force when Britain and the USA, who are struggling to feed the Germans in their zones, discovered the Russians were removing food as reparations.

■ 15,000 **babies** have been born in Liverpool in the first 9 months of this year – more than in the whole of 1945 – earning it the name 'baby boom city'.

14 Thursday

Prime Minister Clement Attlee is to broadcast an **appeal** on Sunday night asking every person in the UK to donate 5s. to a Peoples' Fund to raise £40,000 for a

NOVEMBER

memorial to the late US President **Franklin D Roosevelt** to be erected in Grosvenor Square, London.
■ Norway's revenue is receiving an unexpected boost. Wartime traitors' fines have brought in £2.5 million, most of it paid by people pleading guilty to avoid a public trial.
■ More than 8.5 million pairs of nylon **stockings** will be in the shops next June, and more silk stockings will be available next year.

15 Friday

Modern road design has been so successful at cutting the **accident** rate in Sweden that their methods should be introduced in Britain. The British Road Federation report recommends the construction of elevated and sunken roadways, fly-over bridges and clear road crossings if the British accident rate is to be reduced.
■ The **Nobel Peace Prize** has been awarded to two Americans – Emily Greene Balch (79), the president of the Women's Peace League, and the missionary John R Mott (81). The German poet and novelist, Herman Hesse (69) receives the Nobel Prize for Literature.

16 Saturday

A jet-propelled Lancastrian, the first jet aeroplane to carry passengers from one country to another, flies from London to the Paris Air Show.
■ An anti-whooping cough **vaccine**, used successfully in the USA, is to be tested on 600 Manchester schoolchildren – all volunteers.

17 Sunday

6,000 Manchester transport workers go on **strike** for higher wages. Every bus, train and trolleybus in the city comes to a standstill.
■ Eight British servicemen are killed in Jerusalem as **Jewish terrorists** launch a wave of bombings. In London, Scotland Yard steps up the protection of leading political figures following threats by extremists to extend their terror campaign to Britain.

18 Monday

The world is short of 10 million tons of **grain,** according to the International Emergency Fund Council in Washington, USA. It needs 35 million tons of grain to supply all demands but can provide only 25 million tons.
■ 55 Labour MPs table a motion in the House of Commons calling on the Government to make every effort to 'provide a democratic and constructive Socialist alternative to an otherwise inevitable conflict between American capitalism and Soviet Communism.' It is defeated by 353-0.

19 Tuesday

The BBC will broadcast warnings of **electricity cuts** after radio weather

NOVEMBER

MUM, THERE'S A PLANE IN MY BEDROOM...

The end of 1946 sees a rash of air crashes – and some lucky escapes. On November 19 an RAF Mosquito bomber comes down in flames just 200 yards clear of Kippax, W. Yorks. Both pilot and co-pilot are unhurt. Exactly a month later comes the most spectacular incident (left), when a Railway Air Services Dakota liner lands on top of two houses in South Ruislip, Middx. Again, no-one is injured. On December 30, a Lockheed Constellation, the world's largest airliner, crashes at Shannon Airport, Ireland (right).

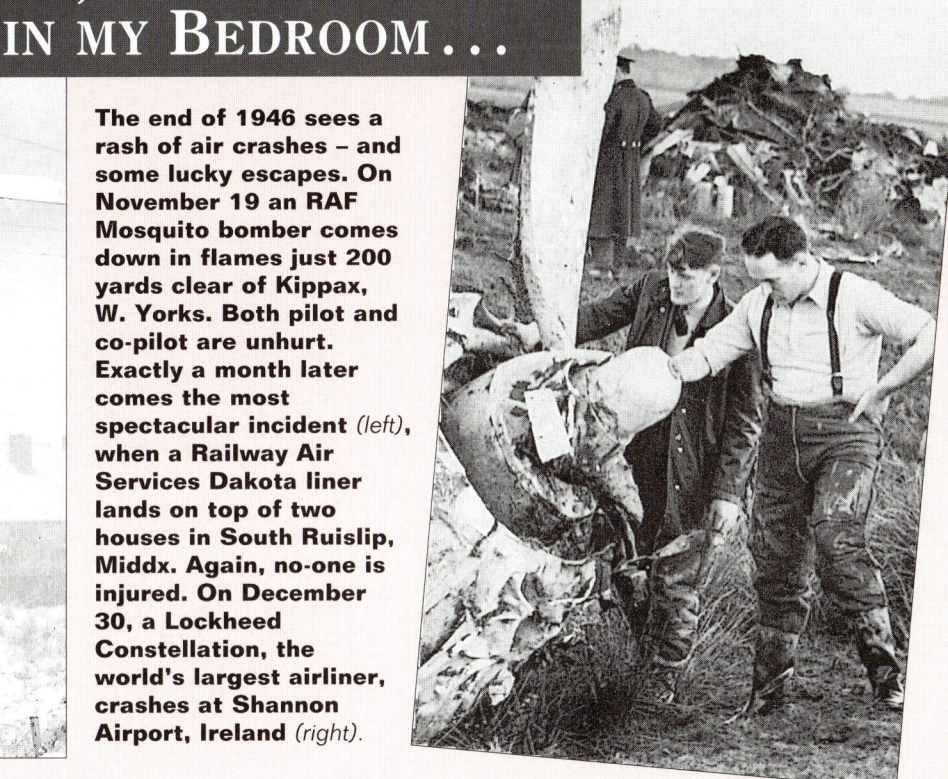

forecasts in future. Consumers are asked to save current to avoid further cuts.
■ The total number of British men and women back in **civilian** life now tops 4 million, according to the latest demob figures issued by the War Office.

20 Wednesday

The US Government will make every effort to maintain **food** shipments to Europe despite the strike of 400,000 miners today.
■ **Baths** in the centre of the city 'where businessmen can revive their leaden energies' are suggested by the Lord Mayor of London, Alderman W. Gregson.
■ The imposition of a **betting tax** would lead to an increase in illegal betting, says the Churches Committee on Gambling.

21 Thursday

Hundreds of tons of parcels are piled up at Paddington Station in London because 3,000 railmen have been working to rule in Great Western goods depots.
■ In Tongking, French Indo-China, **Vietnamese** troops fire on and kill 4 French soldiers investigating the graves of some French and Annamese killed by the Japanese.
■ **Gale warnings** are in force along every mile of Britain's coasts.

22 Friday

Eight RAF men are killed and 11 injured when a bomber landing in the dusk at Locking RAF station nr Weston Super Mare, Somerset, rips the top off a double-decker bus packed with airmen going on weekend leave. The plane, a Boston, **crash-lands** 500yds away without further injury.
■ The US Military Government sends 50,000 tons of **wheat**, flour and oats to help meet the critical shortage in Germany.

NOVEMBER

23 Saturday
New Moon

Following brawls in Tel Aviv, senior officials are discussing the problem of how to curb the growing anger against the Jews among British forces and police in **Palestine**.
- British film producer Lou Jackson has signed Robert Morley to star in his new picture *Ghosts at Berkeley Square*. When the deal was finalised, Morley sent him a telegram which read, 'Best wishes for success of your new picture and heartiest congratulations on securing me to star.'

24 Sunday

While the Rev. Peter Mayhew, Anglo-Catholic vicar of St Aidan's Church, Leeds, preaches his sermon, his 24 **choirboys** in the stalls behind the pulpit are deeply interested – in detective thrillers. Father Mayhew gave them the books because, he says, 'I would rather see boys reading thrillers than being bored by a sermon.'
- The US miners' strike has hit Denmark's coal imports – gas supplies will be cut by half and the country's rail services will cease.

25 Monday

MPs are shocked to find the price of a set lunch in the House of Commons has risen from 1s.6d .to 2s.6d, and set dinners from 2s. to 2s.6d. (à la Carte prices have not changed). No warning had been given.
- Police in Hamburg, Germany, warn people not to drink **illicit spirits** sold by black marketeers. They suspect them of stealing a large quantity of preserving alcohol from jars in the Zoological Institute. The jars contained snakes, lizards, tapeworms and other biological exhibits.

26 Tuesday

A battalion of the Welsh Guards has been ordered to Haifa to await the arrival of the 2,000 ton *Knesset Israel*, the biggest Jewish immigrant ship yet to approach the shores of Palestine. 4,000 immigrants are reported to be on board, and it is feared they will attempt to rush the shore.
- In a broadcast to the nation, Prime Minister Attlee explains the slow-down of **demobilisation** and continuing conscription: 4,400,000 of the 5,100,000 men and women serving on VE Day will have been demobbed by the end of the year. The total remaining under arms will be 1,335,000. The Government fears that if we reduce our strength too much we might endanger our ability to work for world peace.

27 Wednesday

Representatives of 18 countries, including Britain, the Dominions and the USA, but not the USSR, have been meeting in London for the last six weeks to draw up a Trade Charter to prevent another Depression. They agree that each owes it to the others to maintain full employment.

WRITE CLEVER, MR BIRO... A revolutionary new pen hits the market. It can write 200,000 words without refilling, blotting or smudging, and combines a ball point with a tiny capillary tube that holds quick-drying ink. It costs £5.5s, is the invention of Hungarian journalist Ladislao Biro, and is made in Britain.

DECEMBER

28 Thursday

■ The US Navy Department invited bids for the 29,000 ton battleship *Oklahoma* – sunk at Pearl Harbour but later raised for war operations. The highest bid was £11,530 – one offer, sent on a postcard, was 5s.

At the UN in New York, **Sir Hartley Shawcross**, Britain's representative, pledges support to the Russian proposal that not only should the nations ban the use of atomic energy in warfare, but that a special UNO Commission be set up to see that the ban is carried out.

■ In the House of Lords, the **Archbishop of Canterbury** (below) condemns the 'startling brevity' of the marriage ceremony in Registry Offices because it fails to make clear what the ceremony is about and many young people are unaware that they are entering upon a life-long contract.

29 Friday

A full-scale invasion of Britain is planned by Metro-Goldwyn-Mayer, one of Hollywood's major production companies, which starts movie-making in a big way at Elstree Studios, Middlesex, next year. Several big stars have already received tentative sailing orders, among them Spencer Tracy, Walter Pidgeon and Greer Garson.

■ Dividing up the **national debt** of £23,636,520,000, Mr Dalton, Chancellor of the Exchequer, says every one of us owes £482, compared with £149 in 1939.

30 Saturday

US strikers have broken a 27yr-old record. The number of workers on strike so far this year has already exceeded the total of 4,160,000 set in 1919. Man-days lost in the first 10 months of this year totalled 102,525,000.

■ **Herbert Morrison**, Lord President of the Council, warns Northumberland miners that the shortage of coal threatens permanent austerity.

DECEMBER

1 Sunday

Stocking manufacturers fear that when **nylons** do get into the shops they will go straight under the counter.

■ A new daily **steamship** service between Folkestone and Calais opens today, connecting with express trains running to Switzerland.

2 Monday

Britain and America sign a bilateral pact for the merger of their **occupation zones** in Germany. The pact is designed to make the territory self-supporting within 3yrs.

■ With banners flying and led by their village bands, 600,000 **miners** throughout the UK will march to their pitheads on January 1 and nail up plaques announcing that the property from that day belongs to the State.

. . . Aluminium shoes, made from scrapped planes and weighing only 3oz, are being made in Sydney, Australia . . .

3 Tuesday

The Union of Post Office workers is to open a political fund for the first time since 1927 when, under the Trades Disputes Act, civil service organisations were banned from doing so.

■ The wives and children of about 50,000 disabled **pensioners** of the 1914-18 War, not previously eligible, are to receive allowances at a cost of approximately £500,000 a year.

4 Wednesday

A statement from Downing Street says that from now on the award of the Order of the Garter will be made personally by the King and not by recommendation of the Prime Minister – the procedure when the Order was formed in 1349. It coincides with the appointment of 7 new

DECEMBER

Knights of the Garter, including Viscount Montgomery, Viscount Mountbatten and Viscount Alexander.
■ Lord Wavell, Viceroy of India, together with Congress, Moslem and Sikh leaders, arrives in London for talks on India's independence.

5 Thursday

War service has earned **Prince Philip** of Greece priority in his application for British nationality, the Home Secretary, Mr Ede, says in a written reply. Prince Philip became a cadet in the Royal Navy in 1939.
■ When a **jackdaw** at the National Exhibition of Birds at Westminster said raucously, 'Come on, come on,' and chuckled wickedly, Princess Elizabeth turned to Mrs Marjorie Frayne of Doncaster, Yorks, and told her about the parrot the King and Queen brought home with them from Australia. 'The princess said they could never have it in the room when there were visitors,' said Mrs Frayne. 'Apparently, it had belonged to a seaman.'

6 Friday

The talks in London with Indian leaders fail. **Prime Minister Attlee** succeeds in getting all the delegates together but the hour-long meeting brings no solution to India's problems. The Moslem delegates remain adamant in their refusal to take part in India's Constituent Assembly.
■ Not a **turkey** or goose is in the pens at the first pre-Christmas market at Diss in Norfolk, but in the yard of a nearby public house, 20 prime turkeys are sold on the black market for £10 each - more than double the control price.

7 Saturday

A report of the Parliamentary and Scientific Committee calls for the biggest ever expansion of British universities costing £1,000 million in the next 10yrs. An increase from about 55,000 fully qualified scientists to 90,000 is needed, as is a parallel expansion of science education in schools.
■ **Fire** sweeps the 15-storey Winecoff Hotel in Atlanta, Georgia, causing at least 120 deaths. The hotel has no fire escapes or other emergency exits.

8 Sunday
Full Moon

Palestine-based RAF aircraft drop supplies to 1,800 Jewish illegal **immigrants** stranded on the small Mediterranean island Syrina, 500 miles from Haifa, Palestine, in response to an appeal for help from the Jewish Agency. Their ship ran aground trying to run the Royal Navy blockade and the refugees, disembarking in rough seas, lost all their food and supplies.
■ Bombs wreck a Barcelona Youth HQ as the Spanish left wing seeks to call a general strike in protest against government-inspired anti-UN demonstrations for 11 am today. *(See Feb 28, June 24, Nov 3.)*

9 Monday

■ A UN motion recommending members to recall their ambassadors or ministers from **Spain** immediately is carried by 27-7. A further recommendation that if the Franco Government does not end soon the Security Council should consider steps to remedy the situation is adopted by 26-8.
■ Waste paper, bought by a carpenter in Leningrad, Russia, to cover the walls of his flat is found to include the manuscript music score of Tchaikowsky's *Nutcracker* ballet suite.

10 Tuesday

German POWs in Britain may now accept invitations to private houses provided the commander of their camp gives permission. They may also take unescorted walks and

DECEMBER

talk with anyone they meet within a radius of 5 miles of their camp until lighting-up time.
■ **Damon Runyon** (62), author of *Guys and Dolls*, dies in a New York hospital.
■ Conductors walk in front of buses holding lighted newspapers to guide the drivers as a blanket of **fog** descends on London. It also affects Surrey, Birmingham and Manchester.

11 Wednesday

The Big Four (UK, USA, France and USSR) Foreign Ministers agree to sign treaties with Germany's former satellites - Italy, Rumania, Bulgaria, Hungary and Finland – in Paris on February 10. Their deputies will start work on the German Treaty in London in January.
■ **Mr John D Rockefeller** (right) comes to the aid of the UN and offers to buy them a 6-block $8.5 million site on the East River in Manhattan, New York.

12 Thursday

Mr Herbert Morrison (pictured, facing page), Lord President of the Council, says the independent status of the BBC must be preserved, providing it is fair and gives an opportunity to reply.
■ The British Medical Association, representing Britain's **doctors**, refuses to negotiate with the Minister of Health on the operation of the National Health Service. Mr Bevan says he is consulting all the many other interests that will be concerned in the new Health Service.

13 Friday

Orders issued by the Home Office to Local Authorities state that from January 1 **foster parents** will sign an agreement that the children in their care will have their social, mental and emotional needs considered as well as their physical welfare. They are forbidden to injure children. Local Authorities must ensure that a visitor calls at the child's new home at regular short intervals.
■ **Phyllis Calvert**, one of Britain's most popular film stars, has signed a long-term contract with Paramount Pictures for one film a year to be made in the USA.

14 Saturday

The King's **birthday** – he is 51 today.
■ Australia's resolution aimed at restricting the use of the big powers' **veto** in the UN Security Council is passed by the UN General Assembly in New York by 36 to 6, with 11 abstentions. The 6 votes against are all from the Soviet group.
■ A state of bare politeness exists between the Ministry of Food and the *Baptist Times*, since the Ministry sent a Christmas advertisement to the paper giving a recipe for Christmas pudding which included 'a quarter of a pint of rum, ale or stout'. Howls of protest came from their readers. 'To our immense regret, the item slipped through unnoticed,' explains Mr Townley Lord, editor of the *Baptist Times*.

15 Sunday

Pandit Nehru, Vice President of the Indian Interim Government, addressing a mass meeting of over 100,000 people at Benares, India, says, 'whatever form of constitution we decide in the constituent assembly will become the constitution of free India – whether Britain likes it or not.'
■ After an 11-month battle over the World Federation of Trade Unions, the **UN Assembly** in New York votes by 25 to 23 in favour of permitting it to submit questions for the UN Economic Council's Agenda. Britain and USA had opposed special privileges for the WFTU because it would open the door to other non-governmental agencies.
. . . The first snow falls in London. It's 33°F.

DECEMBER

16 Monday

Mr Barnes, Minister of Transport, moves the 2nd reading of the Transport Bill, the most far-reaching measure of nationalisation yet, covering railways, road transport and passenger services, inland waterways and docks and harbours – services which employ almost 6% of the working population.

■ **Seagulls** and starlings are being sold in London as Christmas fare at 3s. each.

■ Another British picture has hit the Hollywood headlines. *Stairway to Heaven*, the US title for *A Matter of Life and Death*, starring David Niven and Roger Livesey, receives rave notices.

17 Tuesday

Bow ties made of **furs** ranging from mole to mink are now being sold in New York, and a man can wear a tie to match his wife's fur coat. Prices start at £6.6s. upwards.

■ The Ministry of Food plans to import a million bottles of **rum** from Jamaica, British Guyana, Trinidad and Barbados. It was all blended in 1943 and will sell at 29s.3d. a bottle.

18 Wednesday

In its survey of the year *Kinematograph Weekly* reports that British films have soared to the top in pulling in the crowds. *The Wicked Lady* is the biggest draw in 1946. Third is *Piccadilly Incident* starring Michael Wilding and Anna Neagle, and in between is *The Bells of St Mary's* starring Ingrid Bergman and Bing Crosby. Top actor is **James Mason** followed by Bing Crosby, Bob Hope, Alan Ladd, Ray Milland, Bette Davis, Anna Neagle and Stewart Granger. J. Arthur Rank announces that British films brought in $8 million to Britain in 1946.

■ Nearly 3 million German, Italian and Japanese POWs are being used to build railways and roads through Siberia, reports *Pravda*, the Russian newspaper.

HELLO AND GOODBYE...

Hello to...
- The Biro
- Bikinis
- The Jitterbug
- The Iron Curtain
- Food shortages
- Welfare State
- Car phones
- United Nations
- IBM Electronic Calculator
- Nylon stockings
- Bananas for London *(far right)*
- Royal Command Film Performance
- The Vespa
- Bread rationing
- British European Airways
- London Heathrow
- The 'People's Car'

Some famous people died in 1946, while the year also spawned some new ideas, crazes... and problems

Goodbye to...
- John Maynard Keynes
- H G Wells
- Damon Runyan
- Goering and other Nazi war criminals
- Austerity – slowly
- The Italian Monarchy
- John Logie Baird
- William S Hart
- W C Field
- George Arliss
- James Mason moves to Hollywood
- GI Brides *(left)*

19 Thursday

The House of Commons votes to nationalise the railways, road transport and the ports. Jubilant Labour MPs sing *The Red Flag* as they queue in the Division lobby. Opposition to the Transport Bill is shown for the first time in this Parliament when over 200 votes are cast against the Government. Altogether 570 MPs (out of the 640 total) vote. 1,000 Opposition amendments are expected *(see 16 Dec)*.

■ In its 'Best in 1946' awards, the National Board of Review of Motion Pictures in New York gives Best Actor to **Laurence Olivier** and Best Film to *Henry V* followed by *Open City, The Best Years of Our Lives, Brief Encounter, A Walk in the Sun, My Darling Clementine, Diary of a Chambermaid, Anna and the King of Siam*.

20 Friday

Birmingham City Electricity Department recommend drastic steps to the Government to save **electricity**, including a 4-day week in industrial and commercial concerns. Today, the country experiences its biggest electricity

DECEMBER

the first time in history, we have brought together mankind in one body to work for peace. Two-thirds of that body are coloured. The other third will have to sit up. They have always been the ruling power – and they still are. For how long, who knows . . .'
■ Technicolour shots of Hitler and Eva Braun bathing in the nude are included in a film of them at play, which the US Army has seized in Bavaria, Germany.

23 Monday

The French military commander in French Indo-China, has ordered his troops at Vinhon to **surrender** to Nationalist forces to avoid a massacre of the French population. A state of undeclared war exists between France and Vietnam.
■ After a film critic announced she was 'the most gorgeous thing yet photographed in Technicolor' in *Salome Where she Danced*, Yvonne de Carlo is appearing in another glamorous role in *Scheherezade of the 1001 Nights*. The Canadian-born star is reported to have ambitions to sing Carmen.

cuts yet – the longest lasted for 1 hr.
■ The **January Sales** are being revived by many stores. There will be fashion bargains at cut prices and cut coupon rates, but no fully-fashioned stockings, underwear or knitted goods which are still scarce.
. . . Fog closes down many parts of Britain. Ice, snow, sleet and rain disrupt road, rail and air services . .

21 Saturday

A major **earthquake** followed by 6 tidal waves devastates 60,000 square miles of southern Japan killing 1,000 and leaving 100,000 homeless.
■ Because they look 'undignified' in the official 'fore-and-aft' hats worn by Bridlington, Yorks, councillors, and the hats spoil their hair, the General Purposes Committee recommends that the town's two women councillors get specially made tricorn hats at £4.11s.5d. each.

22 Sunday

General Smuts, Prime Minister of South Africa, speaking in Pretoria on his return from the UN Assembly in the USA says: 'For

24 Tuesday
Christmas Eve

Hollywood is ending its most disastrous year for 'perfect marriages' with 30 noted couples seeking divorce or separation. Among the stars remarrying in 1946 were Constance Bennett (for the 5th time); Carole Landis, Mary Astor and Gladys George (for the 4th) and Lois Andrews, who is only 22, for the third time.
. . . Two reindeer, with a Laplander in furs as their escort, reach Newcastle-upon-Tyne on their way to London Zoo . . .

25 Wednesday
Christmas Day

W C Fields (66) juggler, film comedian, wise-cracker and Mr Micawber in the film *David Copperfield*, dies in Hollywood.

DECEMBER

■ **A fishy story**: The US National Safety Council reports the story of James Mantakes of Le Grande, Oregon, who was driving across a windy plain with a salmon in the back of his car. Mr Mantakes says the salmon must have got dust in its nose, because it sneezed. Then a grasshopper flew in the window, and the salmon lunged at it. Somehow the salmon landed on Mr Mantakes' lap, and sent his car off the road and into a tree.

26 Thursday
Boxing Day

The film projectors of the Savoy Cinema in Brighton, Sussex start whirring this morning and will continue night and day for 36hrs. They anticipate an audience of late-night workers, people who have been to dances and parties, those who are attracted by the occasion, and any sufferers from insomnia. The film they are showing is, appropriately, *Night and Day* starring Cary Grant.
■ The American actor and ex-marine **Sterling Hayden** is awarded the Silver Star for courage.

27 Friday

The Anglo-Iranian Oil Company and Standard Oil of New Jersey are considering building a £30 million oil pipeline from the Persian Gulf to the eastern Mediterranean to cut out the long voyage by tankers through the Red Sea and the Suez Canal.
■ The Rev. Charles Tuckwell (33), eager to preach in Spokane, Washington, hundreds of miles from his home, couldn't get a seat on a plane or train, so he stole a plane at Tacoma aerodrome. He then got lost in a snowstorm, made a forced landing on an Indian reservation, and hitch-hiked to Spokane, where he preached against sin. When he was arrested for stealing the plane, Rev. Tuckwell asked, 'Is spreading the word of God a sin? It was a fine sermon, if I do say so myself.'

28 Saturday

Field Marshal Lord Montgomery, has accepted an invitation to visit Moscow next month to study the Red Army's methods.
■ Four farmhands at Roanne, France, are arrested on charges of throwing a **bomb** into a tobacco shop. They told the police they were fed up with the delay in distributing their tobacco rations.

29 Sunday

The **Archbishop of York**, Dr C F Garbett, asks the members of his diocese to think over what they spend on amusements and compare it with what they give each week to God, and urges them to attend Church at least once a week.
■ **Terrorist** outrages continue in Palestine. A British major at Natanya, and three NCOs from Tel Aviv and Rischon are seized and flogged.

30 Monday

The Players Union threatens to greet the New Year with a strike as they are not satisfied with the Football League's proposed new wage offer for full-time players of £11 maximum and £6 minimum for the 1947-1948 playing season (see Nov 4).
■ **Margaret Truman** (22), the only child of the US President, has astonished Washington society by turning her back on the brilliant social season to live in New York and study singing. Her ambition is to be an opera singer.

31 Tuesday

The UN Atomic Energy Commission adopts the American plan for the international control of atomic power. Under the plan, no government will have the right to obstruct control or inspection by the use of the veto or otherwise.
■ New York film critics declare British actors **Laurence Olivie**r and **Celia Johnson** Best Actor and Actress of 1946 for their roles in *Henry V* and *Brief Encounter* respectively.

SPITFIRE QUIZ, *on page 29.*
The Spitfire is pictured in the foreground